Whole Language: Practical Ideas

MAYLING CHOW

LEE DOBSON

MARIETTA HURST

JOY NUCICH

Pippin Publishing Limited

KH

Copyright © 1991 by Pippin Publishing Limited
150 Telson Road
Markham, Ontario
L3R 1E5

Designed by John Zehethofer
Edited by Elma Schemenauer
Typesetting by Colborne, Cox & Burns
Printed and bound by The Alger Press

Canadian Cataloguing in Publication Data

Main entry under title:
   Whole language : practical ideas

(The Pippin teacher's library; 1)
Includes bibliographical references.
ISBN 0-88751-032-9

1. Reading (Elementary) - Language experience approach.
2. English language - Composition and exercises - Study and
teaching (Elementary).   3. Language experience approach in
education.   I. Chow, Mayling.   II. Series.

LB1576.W46 1991   372.6044   C91-094104-1

ISBN 0-88751-032-9

10 9 8 7 6 5 4 3 2 1

08/26/08

CONTENTS

We dedicate this book to our families.
We could not have completed it
without their generous support.

. . . .

FOREWORD

We have gradually developed the program described in this book. Upon reflection, there were many influences that contributed significantly to our professional growth over time. We worked together in the same school for several years. Some of us were teaching in classrooms. Some were teaching reading, writing, and English in learning centers. There was an open section of the school that brought us together. We taught side by side, sharing space, materials, ideas, and, at times, even students. As we worked closely together, sharing problems and successes, we developed strong feelings of mutual respect.

Our school was located in an area of the city where most families were socioeconomically disadvantaged. The slow rate of progress of our students concerned us greatly; we felt we simply weren't connecting with their knowledge or their interests. Our students seemed to be finding their schooling less and less relevant with time.

During this period we became aware of the support for Noam Chomsky's exciting new theory that young children develop oral language by inducing increasingly complex rules. This implied that young children actually control the learning of oral language. We found extensions of this theory, which proposed that children learn written language in a similar manner. Our dissatisfaction with our students' progress, together with this exciting research, led us to reflect further on our practices and study. We attended workshops and courses together, discussing our findings with each other. We recommended readings to each other and shared our reflections on them. We quietly tried small changes without fanfare, not knowing how they would go or how they would be received.

1

The support of a new administrator encouraged us to incorporate more actively and openly the stimulating ideas we were discussing. The pace and extent of our innovations quickened, as did the response of our students. The exploration of student writing provided a major impetus for change. We would regularly congregate in the staff room to celebrate our students' most recent discoveries or successes. Most of our socializing in the staff room consisted of "talking shop."

Parents and other teachers were drawn into our excitement and we jointly began to provide workshops. Many of us by this time were working on advanced degrees. We were honing our thoughts and beliefs as we simultaneously planned the workshops and pursued our professional writing. We were applying for and receiving grants to do classroom research. Drafting and revising applications for grants in writing led us to refine our thinking further.

The more we read, studied, discussed, and learned, the more we recognized the valuable strategies our students already had and the competencies they were developing. The cycle fed itself as we learned to evaluate progress as informed observers. We gained expertise over time, gradually articulating our beliefs, developing and refining our practices, and examining them for consistency. We do not have the single best way to nurture the learning of our students, nor is our work complete. We are constantly learning. The key has been to find a way that works for us and our students. We hope this book will help you do the same.

We gratefully acknowledge permission granted by the Canadian Council of Teachers of English to reprint an excerpt from the following journal article: Crowhurst, M.: "Prerequisites for teaching writing: What the writing teacher needs to know and be." *Canadian Journal of English Language Arts,* 11(2). (1988) 5–12.

We take great pride in acknowledging the inspiration and support of a number of colleagues who have helped us with our professional growth and the development of this program. We wish to thank Shirley Brunke, Spencer Cotton, Rachel Duncan, Anne Forester, Lenore Hampton, Chuck Jordan, Margaret Reinhard, Gwen Smith, Tom Stack, Linda Stickley, and Beth Trask.

. . . .

PRINCIPLES AND

RESPONSIBILITIES

Recent Research as a Basis for New Practices

Over the last few years, we have initiated new practices that reflect changing beliefs about the teaching and learning of literacy. We were inspired by the work of several researchers in the field of oral and written language development. The findings of these researchers complemented each other, and strongly influenced our ideas and the development of our program. Smith (1979) said "children learn to read by reading" and Graves (1983) found that "children want to write. . . ." Goodman (1978) developed a sophisticated qualitative analysis of oral reading strategies, which revealed that all readers use the same complex process. He characterized learning to read not as a progression of parts to the whole but as a progression of successive approximations of proficient reading (1972).

Read (1971) similarly documented the systematic nature of preschool children's developing knowledge of English phonology. Our initial purpose was to set up classroom environments so that all children could participate in literacy events. In this context both students and teachers see literacy as meaningful. They participate in literacy for real purposes and with enjoyment. They discuss their literacy activities. They welcome student-initiated literacy. And they treat all literacy efforts seriously (Hall, 1987).

Working from this perspective and Marietta Hurst's ideas on emergent literacy and principles for the nurturing environment, we began to organize curricula in a new way. Within a framework of shared and independent literacy activities, we used literature as a medium of instruction. We also explored the possibility that all children can write in their own way at their own level. As we

3

continued to innovate, we reflected on the compatibility of our practices with the underlying theory. In this book we present the practices we have developed over twelve years of working together. But they are not our last word. We believe that we must continue to observe, read, write, and reflect, and thus remain open to further evaluation and refinements.

The Learning Environment

In the course of her studies as a graduate student, Marietta Hurst surveyed literature on the learning of oral and written language. She was searching for general principles present in environments found to nurture language learning. Her initial principles gave a theoretical basis to our practices. Our practices, in turn, have led Marietta to refine her principles. We refer to the guiding principles whenever we are unsure of our direction, even in our day-to-day interactions with students. These principles structure the learning environment in our classrooms and have proved to be an important and valid guide in deciding upon curricula and evaluation of student learning. We believe they are a significant factor in the success of our Whole Language program. Following is a listing of our basic principles of instruction.

1. Provide a warm social setting.
   Language learning is a distinctly social task that requires learners to actively form and test hypotheses. Therefore we must provide respect, acceptance, and trust in learning so that students feel safe enough to take risks and reveal their thinking.

2. Immerse learners in a literate environment.
   Children learn to speak and to understand their oral language through using it and being immersed in it. In a similar way, we have found that our students readily learn to read and write when we surround them with genuine, purposeful written language and invite them to participate in its use.

3. Accept and encourage successive approximations of literacy.
   When we trust and encourage students to learn according to their own natural strategies and rates of progress, and when we respond in a way that makes sense to them, we see that their progress follows a path of successive approximations. In turn, we come to trust them to assume even more control over their own learning.

4

4. Expect self-selection of materials and of topics.
   When students choose their own reading and writing, they see literacy as purposeful, meaningful, and under their control. We tell our students that we expect them to handle this choice intelligently, and they do.

5. Respond to intended meaning as the absolute priority.
   Unless we keep meaning as the absolute priority, we distort literacy, falsify its purpose, and change its very nature. Such distortions make literacy learning difficult rather than easy.

6. Emphasize the process rather than the product.
   When we recognize that learners progress through successive approximations, we conclude that the process of learning is much more important than the conventionality of individual products. Students profit only from teaching that they can incorporate into their current understanding.

7. Expect hypothesis-testing and self-correction.
   By closely observing learners, we see them forming and testing increasingly sophisticated hypotheses about reading and writing. We use their errors and self-corrections as evidence of good strategies and thinking, which we can applaud and celebrate.

8. Set high standards while expecting a developmental progression along a learning continuum.
   When we know how learners develop in general, then we can observe students' progress and assist them along the way. We set high standards, which they achieve by systematically developing more complex strategies and understandings of the rules and conventions of literacy.

9. Evaluate individually and longitudinally.
   Once we recognize that learning is developmental, we realize that evaluation must be individual and must take place at regular intervals. It must also be integral to the interactions between student and teacher, and be consistent with the goals of the program. We want to enhance rather than block student progress and demonstrate techniques for effective self-evaluation.

Guidelines for Sharing Responsibilities

When we create classrooms based on these principles, we find there is a necessary shift in what we expect from students and how we share responsibilities with them. We establish guidelines for students from the beginning, so that we do not compromise either our high expectations or our firm control of the classroom. The first questions are, "Who is in charge? And of what?"

We say to students, "You are in charge of yourself, but I am in charge of the room. I can't allow you to make decisions that disrupt others." We must manage the classroom in such a way that all students have the opportunity to learn. We know we are succeeding when our classrooms have the purposeful hum of people at work.

We set up the environment, but our students have to assume the responsibility for learning. We make this division of responsibility clear by saying, "I can't get into your head to make you learn. You have to get down to work, and then I can help you."

Talk about the process of learning is ongoing. We let students in on our own thinking by explaining our choices and giving our reasons. We also ask students to articulate what they're doing by asking, "How did you do that? How did you know to do it that way? What have you learned?" This kind of talk, from one learner to another, permeates the program.

After establishing who is in charge of what, our second question is, "What standard of work is acceptable?"

As teachers, we have the responsibility of making sure students put out their best efforts. But we look for evidence of thinking and problem-solving rather than of students having memorized predigested information. If we don't find such evidence, we give students a nudge, or even a push. However, we observe the results of every nudge or push carefully, reflecting on student response in order to evaluate our judgment calls. We ask ourselves, "Am I challenging this student to be the best s/he can be?" (or) "Am I being overly ambitious for this student and thereby discouraging him or her from developing his or her own strategies?" (or) "Am I accepting less than this student's best effort and therefore allowing him or her to rest on his or her laurels?"

Each person needs to know that what s/he does matters; that we teachers care enough to insist that work is of the highest possible quality.

To know when to interfere and when to hold back is the trick. We need to know what each individual student understands and what s/he can do with that understanding. We need to know what students who are operating at a similar level of development typically understand and do. Then it is a matter of judgment gained from personal observations and the shared experiences of colleagues and other educational thinkers. Our hope for this book is that it adds to that store of knowledge, which is critical to the development of teacher judgment.

Teachers' and students' responsibilities tend to mirror each other, and so we set them out in parallel form.

T = TEACHERS' RESPONSIBILITIES
S = STUDENTS' RESPONSIBILITIES

T: To inspire students with the confidence that they can learn to write by writing and to read by reading.
S: To produce writing and reading.

T: To understand and sensitively observe how students' writing and reading develop. To expect a developmental progression of successive approximations in which students induce the rules and conventions of written language.
S: To become aware that writing and reading develop from their own efforts.

T: To act as a genuine audience to the intended meanings of students' writing and reading.
S: To share the meanings of their writing and reading.

T: To give students control and ownership of their writing and reading; its level, pace, and content, while setting high standards.
S: To take control and ownership of their writing and reading; its level, pace, and content by choosing their own topics and materials.

T: To coach and give students information as to their progress and accomplishments. To foster an awareness of their tacit understandings and strategies.
S: To develop strategies to make conscious sense of print for themselves.

7

T: To emphasize the learning process rather than the product. To expect students to use their prior knowledge and oral language competency to induce the rules and conventions of written language through experimentation.

S: To bring their prior knowledge and oral language competency to make sense of print.

T: To emphasize the content rather than the form. To value and accept all students' personal expressions and interpretations as presented. To provide ample demonstrations and regular time for students to experience and explore a variety of genres, topics, styles, forms, and mechanics of reading and writing.

S: To risk error as they experiment with solving problems of selection, style, form, and the conventions and mechanics of reading and writing.

T: To establish where individuals are on the written language learning continuum in order to make decisions on appropriate demonstrations and interactions with them. To individualize and focus teaching on aspects that students are ready to incorporate into their work.

S: To make connections between what they know and what they encounter, including print in the environment and teacher demonstrations.

We hope the ideas we present in this book will assist you, as teachers, to reflect on your present teaching program. We also hope we can stimulate you to try new ideas and activities. In the next chapter we describe learning strategies children already have when they come to school and the parallels we see between oral and written language learning. This information gives direction to our program. We also describe the framework we use to organize curricula. Within this structure we expect teachers to use their own experience, interest, and judgment to develop their own potential and that of their students.

SETTING THE
STAGE

Preschoolers as Highly Efficient Language Learners

Young preschoolers accomplish the highly complex task of learning oral language with unmatched efficiency. They display boundless confidence and initiative as they assume responsibility for their own learning. They learn to take turns in conversation, to listen and understand as well as to speak, and to adjust their responses in turn. They learn to engage the attention of their listeners and to enlist listeners' collaboration in making and negotiating joint meaning. They pose endless questions and pursue countless conversations in their wish to check out or confirm their hypotheses. If the hypotheses are disconfirmed, preschoolers form and test additional ones. They actually learn language as they use it. They learn by doing.

What is it that parents and other care givers do so well, to foster this marvelous growth in young children's learning? Parents are masters at providing the kind of nurturing environment in which children are confident enough to risk error and reveal ignorance without fear of censure. When parents willingly look through the form of preschoolers' language to reach its meaning, they are according the children considerable respect. They respond to their understanding of their children's intention, appropriately negotiating this meaning further. Parents connect, confirm, and collaborate with their children's ideas, applauding successive approximations and projecting confidence. Yet the setting is far from *laissez-faire*. Parents constantly raise their expectations but still manage to keep these within their children's grasp.

In their early years, our students have developed effective learning strategies that have served them magnificently in learning oral language. They have achieved an impressive competence in a minimum of time. In essence they have made sense of oral language for themselves. As well, they have already learned much about written language through their immersion in environmental print. They also know that society attaches considerable importance to the use of written language.

How can we turn our backs on this optimal learning system and setting? Are we not forever puzzled and devastated when we hear of lively, curious, keen youngsters being turned off learning? We need to respect and learn from the shining example of the home. We must leave the control of their learning in the hands of the children and encourage them to capitalize on their strengths. We must recognize their competency and connect with it. We must inspire them, not only to have faith in their powerful strategies, but also to continue to develop and refine them. We have documented and firmly believe that young children of preschool and school entry age can learn literacy efficiently in a manner that is quite comparable to the way they learned oral language.

Parallels in the Development of Oral and Written Language

When children speak they use whatever they know, particularly of language, to communicate their meaning. In turn, their listeners use the entire context of the situation to jointly work out the meaning the speakers intend to convey. We can closely observe and analyze the development of children's language over time. At every stage children use language systematically. By studying their errors we see the highly intelligent strategies and hypotheses they are forming and testing. Errors made in language learning rarely become habit-forming. If we reject errors as "wrong," we also unintentionally reject the good thinking contained in them. This hinders rather than fosters growth.

We need to celebrate the sound strategies and thinking our students are tackling. This will encourage them to pursue and refine such strategies and thought processes. When we place students in a supportive writing environment, we see that they use all their prior knowledge, including their knowledge of oral and written language, to experiment and explore, developing strategies to compose and transcribe their messages. When we look closely at our students' writing over time, we see that it too develops systematically. Parallels in the development of oral and written language appear in the following chart.

Successive Approximations Towards the Conventional	
Oral Language	**Written Language**
babbling	scribbling
repeated sounds (*da-da-da*)	cursive-like scribble or letter-like symbols
telegraphic sentences (*me cookie*)	telegraphic spellings (*IHVAHS — I have a house.*)
overgeneralized rules (*I goed to the store.*)	overgeneralized rules (*GHO* — abstracted from the spelling of *ghost* and generalized to spell *go*.)
(*My feets hurt.*)	(*TR WZ A BT A FL HS — There was a beautiful house.* An initial experiment with word separation.)

Students learn to write by reading and writing and to read by writing and reading. The processes are constantly intertwined, and nurture one another. Students develop and refine their strategies in use as we immerse them in both processes. Shared reading and writing situations provide opportunities for us to demonstrate the processes in use and to invite and support the active participation of students in the processes. The shared situation

Four Components of the Organizational Framework

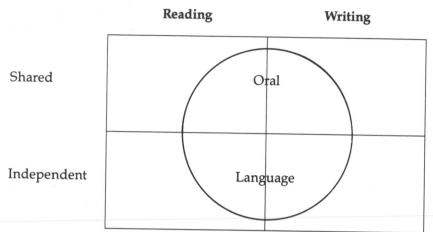

may involve a teacher and a student, a teacher and a small group, or a teacher and a class.

When students engage in independent reading and writing, they are working on operating the processes for themselves by exploring the development and integration of their strategies. The path that young learners take as they explore transcription in writing suggests that they are reinventing the spelling system to make sense of it for themselves. We closely observe students' efforts towards literacy. We thus gain an understanding of their thinking, the progress of their strategies over time, and ways we can work more effectively with them.

We continually provide opportunities for all students to engage in literacy activities but those activities, in themselves, do not guarantee progress in learning. The learning takes place in the discussions, and by this we mean oral language interactions, which are an integral part of all four literacy components. The quality of discussion in classrooms directly affects students' learning. We often refer to these discussions as conferences, and they accompany and highlight all reading and writing activities. They may involve the whole class, small groups, or individual students. Initially we spend a lot of time modeling appropriate responses to students' work. Mayling Chow selected and priorized four action verbs that underlie our intentions in this regard. They are *connect, confirm, celebrate,* and *extend.* In the following chapters, we talk about how these terms keep us on track in our conferences with students. In all such interactions, we focus attention on comprehension, and challenge students' ability to solve their own problems of form. Thinking, reasoning, listening, and speaking are integral to this holistic approach.

The Focus on Meaning

We consciously arrange situations so that students focus on the communicative functions of reading and writing. Throughout all literacy activities, we expect them to attend to, reason about, and reflect on meaning by asking themselves, "What does this mean to me? How does it fit in with what I already know?" Naturally, each person responds in his or her own way to such open-ended questions. There is no one correct answer.

We direct our students to go beyond surface considerations and examine the deeper meaning in a piece of writing. Such directives occur throughout this book in situation-specific examples. But we list them here as well, by category, along with stimulating questions that are useful for teachers to have "on the tip of the tongue."

1. Identify the main idea of a communication. (What can we learn from this book? Did someone in the story learn a lesson?)

2. Make inferences based on information received and their own knowledge of the world. (The story talks about _____. What do you think the author was trying to say to us?)

3. Predict events/contents, giving reasons for choice. (What do you think will happen? Why?)

4. Elaborate and expand on their own meaning and the meaning of others. (Tell me more about _____. *or* Elaine, I'd like you to respond to Michael's ideas.)

5. Compare and contrast stories, themes, styles. (What does this story or idea or illustration remind you of?)

6. Ask questions. (Was there anything you were wondering about? If the author were here, what questions might you ask him or her?)

7. Evaluate products and procedures. (Do you think the author was successful in getting the point across? What part of the story do you like best? Why?)

8. Consider future investigations. (How can we follow up today's reading/writing?)

We organize curricula in a way that enables students to experience each of the four components every day. At the core of everything we do is oral language. It is the vehicle by which we make meaning from our literacy activities. In turn, reading and writing stimulate the development of oral language. We recognize that writing, reading, listening, and speaking are all composing processes; language users are in the business of creating meaning.

Each of the next four chapters describes a component and gives examples of our ideas in action. Although we separate these components for organizational purposes, they are not mutually exclusive. They all overlap and interconnect. What is happening in any one category always affects the others.

SHARED READING

A Variety of Experiences and Activities

We plan a great variety of daily experiences, which immerse students in actual reading. As we do so, we demonstrate and coach the multiplicity of strategies involved, focusing on a number of aspects:

1. Bringing background knowledge to reading.
2. Predicting structure and events.
3. Confirming or disconfirming predictions.
4. Encouraging discussion and validating personal interpretations of meaning.
5. Developing a balanced use of the interacting language cue systems (pages 88–97).

This daily routine stimulates participation in all the other literacy experiences of students. We usually direct shared reading activities ourselves and involve the whole class in participation. We present many and varied quality reading experiences, looking for enjoyment and interest for students and ourselves as we work together to create meaning from text.

Steps to Successful Shared Reading Experiences

1. CHOOSING READING SELECTIONS

First we have to choose the reading we share with our students. Our first consideration is to find a selection that draws students' attention and activates their prior knowledge. Most important is the quality of the selection. Quality is hard to define but it certainly involves the following factors: the author's style, the sound and suitability of the language, the clarity of the storyline, the organization of detail and information, the validity of the theme, the authenticity of information, the setting and characters, the selection's cohesion, and the quality of the illustrations, if any, and how they work with the text.

Sometimes certain selections work better with one group of students than with another. The reasons may be the selections' familiarity, relevance, and appeal to the students, or students' experience with the underlying concepts. For young readers we often choose selections that have rhyme, rhythm, and refrain. Young readers can use these elements to guide their predictions of content, and to support them in their independent reading.

Because we also wish to widen students' experience and challenge their thinking, we select a variety of topics, forms, styles, and genres. We offer fiction including illustrated storybooks, novels, songs, poems, chants, and drama. We offer non-fiction including letters, articles, expository text, biographies, and reports.

At times we choose readings that initiate and develop certain themes or concepts, which are then integrated with other aspects of the curriculum.

 *

Do not restrict yourself and the students to certain sources and choices of reading material. Read widely, and read material you like.

2. INTRODUCING THE READING.

We introduce the reading by connecting with students' understanding and background knowledge. We wish to initiate a discussion that gets their ideas flowing, so that they build on each other's ideas as well as developing their own. Such discussion activates thinking, arouses interest, and connects *what is known* with *what can be discovered*. Thus we create opportunities to compose meaning, a strategy common to both reading and writing (with the further advantage of acting as a rehearsal for future independent writing).

*We have used this "STOP" symbol throughout the book to alert you to an aspect of the subject we particularly want to draw to your attention and emphasize.

The authors.

Our introductions focus on a significant aspect of the reading selection. One technique is to display the cover or introductory material of a storybook and ask students to predict what the story may be about. This strategy is particularly effective with a book such as *The Ghost-Eye Tree* (Martin and Archambault, 1985) because the bare black tree, the yellow moon, and the dark blue background on the cover page evoke a feeling of ghostly deeds.

When introducing a modern fairytale such as *Petronella* (Williams, 1973), we might brainstorm for characteristics of fairytales and encourage students to use this knowledge to predict plot and style. (See Weaver, 1988, pages 147–153, for a complete treatment of this story.) In all such discussions we expect students to give reasons for their predictions, to suggest alternatives, and to refine their predictions as a story unfolds.

We select stories that students can compare in terms of theme, setting, characters, plot, or topic. We contrast several versions of the same story, or several books by the same author or illustrator. In such lessons we begin with the books or versions students already know and progress from there.

For non-fiction reading we follow a similar routine. Initially we brainstorm for ideas and knowledge of the subject area, topic, and content. We consider *what we know* and *what we want to find out*. We graphically represent our findings in categorized lists or in a webbing format with the topic as a sun and *what we know* as encircling planets (page 74). Later on, we may use a distinctive color of chalk or felt pen to show that we have verified our initial ideas and to add *what we have found out*.

Children internalize such routines. We don't need to spend a lot of time introducing every story. If we do, students may not experience enough reading and we may interfere with our main goal — our students' assuming control over their own reading.

3. THE READING ITSELF

We read selections aloud ourselves or involve students in oral reading. We do choral readings of prose, poetry, songs, and refrains, often using Big Books. The fact that all students can see and follow the large-size print in these books promotes enjoyable reading practice.

When we read to young students, we demonstrate book-handling and show how print works. We hold books up and point to the print as we read, thereby demonstrating the left to right format and the relationship of spoken words to written text. When we follow this routine, we are careful not to destroy the cohesion of the story. Students also enjoy taking roles and reading the dialogue of their characters as in readers' theater. (See Walker and Walker, 1989, for readers' theater scripts.) We consider the experience of our readers, the audience, and the nature of the material when making our choice of presentation. The possibilities are limited only by our imagination.

We read many uncomplicated books straight through, without interruption or interpretation. On the other hand, some storybooks and novels are more complicated, so we pause at strategic points and ask for interpretation and prediction. For example, we ask, "What has happened in the story so far? What does it mean? What might we expect next?" Similarly we ask questions in response to non-fiction readings; for example, "What have we learned? What does that mean? What else do we need to find out?" We expect students to use the context of story and illustrations, and sometimes grammar and wording, to predict meaning. We always recognize and applaud the good thinking their participation reveals.

We read picture books with older students as well as with younger ones. There are many wonderful illustrated books whose stories involve concepts and vocabulary especially suitable for older children. These storybooks enable students to hear the sound of expressive, complex language and to appreciate finely drawn illustrations. Illustrations are an important source of information for all students, but particularly for less experienced readers. Such readers include those for whom English is a second language.

Students' independent writing can become a part of shared reading. In this case we prepare the class to listen to student material during "Authors' Time." We expect them to respond to the writing as if it were commercially published.

Reading must be enjoyable. Take care not to spoil the impact (kill the story) by interrupting too frequently or for too long.

Our goal is to confirm and then extend students' ideas and understanding. Thus we arrange discussions so that students put their understanding into words, as individuals and as a group, and celebrate what has been learned. We ask open-ended questions to challenge students to go beyond present thinking and elaborate on other aspects of the reading (pages 48 and 49). We often represent student responses graphically on chart paper or chalkboard, and provide opportunities for reflection and evaluation (pages 20–25).

Structuring Student Responses

We encourage students to structure their responses to reading in the following ways.

1. They take turns retelling the plot in their own words, without prompting. We expect them to have internalized the main points of the story; we are not testing their memory for details.

Hints:
- Paraphrase or recapitulate students' offerings for clarification.
- Involve many students in the retelling.
- Use information already given to ask for further elaboration.
- Try to resolve any difference by going over what has been recounted so far, rather than consulting the book.

2. They compare stories or versions of stories, reflecting on similarities and differences and adding written information to charts (page 21).
3. They identify the problems (troubles) in the story and how the characters attempted to solve them. This activity focuses attention on story structure and main events, and may eventually lead to summary statements (pages 22–23).
4. They recognize "the lesson," which is the main point or theme of a selection. We want students to realize that authors have reasons for writing as they do. They may be trying to affect readers' thinking, feeling, knowledge, or attitudes. We discuss authors' intentions and story lessons with students at all grade levels, even if they have difficulty putting such abstract ideas into words.

5. Students map plot lines and show character development through sociograms and other diagrams (pages 24, 75). Varied responses are described in *Children's Literature in the Reading Program* (Cullinan, 1987) and *Literacy Through Literature* (Johnson and Louis, 1990). The trick is to focus on the response that best illuminates the theme(s) of a particular story.

Students respond to poems and plays in a similar fashion. The question is, "What does it mean?" This is an open-ended question. We must ask for and accept students' interpretations and their rationale. Students respond to non-fiction by identifying important information, categories of information, points of view, arguments, and supporting details.

Once students demonstrate their awareness of what we are seeking to accomplish in our comprehension routines and the procedure we follow, we ask them to respond independently or in small peer groups. Students meet the challenge particularly well in group discussion.

1. Always make students accountable for their answers and remember to celebrate good thinking.
2. Allow ample time for many demonstrations of responding to literature before you expect students to work in this way on their own or in peer groups. This holds true for students at all grade levels. Learning the process is more important than a single outcome.

Examples of Shared Reading of Fiction

COMPARING VERSIONS OF FAMILIAR STORIES

1. SELECT: *Chicken Little* (Kellogg, 1985).
2. INTRODUCE: The traditional version of this story is familiar to most children. Ask them what they know about it, obtaining as many details as possible. Usually the animal helpers are eaten by a crafty fox, but the types of animals and their responses vary. Have children talk about the many variations they know.
3. READ: Have the children clustered close to you, able to see the lines of print and the illustrations. Display the book, moving your finger along the line of print you are reading. To invite participation, hesitate on the repetition of the refrain. Probably

children will spontaneously join in, predicting the next word or phrase. Thus they see how print works and begin to develop their own reading strategies. On a second reading you might assign roles and have children play, or read, the parts of the animals.

4. RESPOND: Compare this version of the story with traditional ones. Make a chart of similarities and differences. Collect as many versions as possible (including versions written as plays), introduce them, and add more information to the chart. Make this collection of books available for independent reading. Suggest that some pupils may wish to write their own versions of the story. The K, 1, 2 class of Joy Nucich composed the following chart. The children had so many ideas that we have reproduced only part of it.

Comparison of two versions of *Chicken Little*

Stephen Kellogg Version	Traditional Tale
Fox is caught by police.	Fox gets away with eating animals.
C.L. (Chicken Little) is hit by an acorn.	By a seed.
They enter a truck.	A cave.
C.L. stays and yells.	C.L. runs away.
Animals wear clothes (illustrations).	No clothes.
Go to tell the police.	Go to tell the king.
Uses big words in the story.	Uses simple words.
C.L. has grandchildren.	No grandchildren.

Students can also engage in drama by taking on the roles of the characters in either or both versions, and making up new characters. They can then respond naturally to each other, in role, creating their own version (Verriour, 1989).

1. SELECT: *The Unicorn and the Lake* (Mayer, 1982).
2. INTRODUCE: Ask the students to examine the cover illustration and to predict what the story might be about. Key questions to ask are: "What do unicorns generally symbolize in our literature? What can a title tell us about a story?" Remind students that most plot lines evolve from some problem or problems that need to be solved before a story comes to a conclusion. Then ask them to predict what problems may occur in this story.
3. READ: Read the story, stopping whenever clarification is necessary or when opportunities arise for further predictions. Use pictorial as well as textual cues. At the point when the serpent is introduced, ask students what it may symbolize. Ask what coming events may occur now that good and evil are both on the scene.
4. RESPOND: First ask students to share story problems they have identified. Accept all responses and write them on the chalkboard or chart paper but, at the same time, expect students to provide a rationale for their choices. After some experience with this routine, students come to realize that there is more than one way of interpreting a story and they do not have to come up with the one "correct" answer. At this point students may evaluate the responses and come to a group consensus as to which one(s) best represent(s) the major problem(s) on which the story rests.

   Second ask students to establish whether the story problems are resolved and, if so, in what way. Again, write their answers down. Students arrive at their conclusions through consensus and negotiate how they wish to have them stated.

   Third ask if any characters in the story learned a lesson. If students respond in the affirmative, ask if we can generalize this into a lesson all can benefit from. If no lesson was learned, ask how we, as readers, can learn from this story. Again, take all answers that students can substantiate. Discuss and agree on which lesson(s) best represent(s) group opinion.

●

Teachers need to spend a lot of time accepting all answers before they begin to narrow the possibilities down to one or two key story problems. Students need to know that their thinking is valued and respected, even when it differs from the majority opinion.

Once older students are comfortable with this activity, they can easily discuss "plot" (story problem and solution) and "theme" (lesson), because they now have a framework that enables them to write in a very focused way.

The Unicorn and the Lake
- by Marie Lorne

Story Problem:
1) There was a drought and the animals were dying
2) The snake put poison in the water

Solution:
1) The unicorn went to the top of mountain and put his horn in the clouds and the rain fell.
2) The unicorn put his horn in the lake and the water started to ~~be~~ clear up and became fresh

Lesson:
Help other people who need help. In the story, the unicorn helped the animals even though they forgot about him.

RECOGNIZING AND ANALYZING PLOT LINES

1. SELECT: *Perseus and Medusa* (Naden, 1981).
2. INTRODUCE: Ask students if they know anything about the two people named in the title. Key points to bring out are the story's origins in Greek mythology and the fact that Medusa is connected with ugliness. Discuss other well known characters and tales of this mythology including Zeus and the heroes. Have students make notes of the major events as the story is read (they do not have a copy themselves).
3. READ: Pause at intervals to elaborate on points specific to Greek mythology (for example, the role of oracles). Encourage predictions by asking questions such as, "What will the king do now?" Allow time for student-initiated discussion.
4. RESPOND: Ask students to contribute one event each and place it on a continuum according to its order of appearance in the

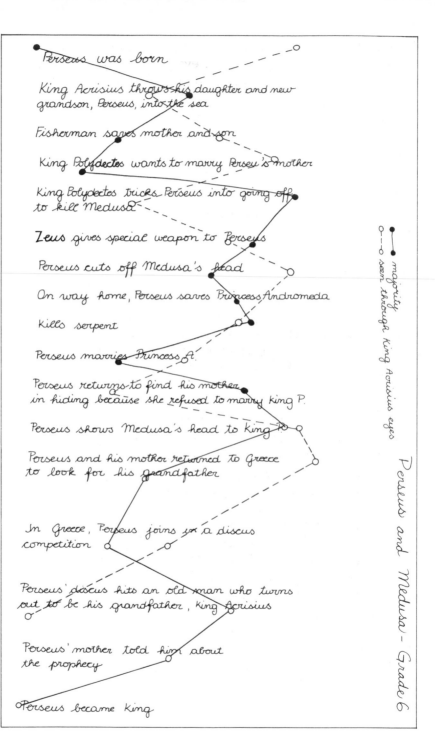

Perseus was born

King Acrisius throws his daughter and new grandson, Perseus, into the sea

Fisherman saves mother and son

King Polydectes wants to marry Perseus's mother

King Polydectes tricks Perseus into going off to kill Medusa

Zeus gives special weapon to Perseus

Perseus cuts off Medusa's head

On way home, Perseus saves Princess Andromeda

Kills serpent

Perseus marries Princess A.

Perseus returns to find his mother in hiding because she refused to marry king P.

Perseus shows Medusa's head to King P.

Perseus and his mother returned to Greece to look for his grandfather

In Greece, Perseus joins in a discus competition

Perseus' discus hits an old man who turns out to be his grandfather, King Acrisius

Perseus' mother told him about the prophecy

Perseus became King

•——• majority
o——o seen through King Acrisius eyes

Perseus and Medusa – Grade 6

24

story. (Leave lots of room between events so that you can add more detail as the discussion evolves.) When all events are written on the chart, ask students to identify which event created the most tension. Discuss "climax." Accept all answers but go with the majority vote. Assign a dot to each event and make a plot line that eventually leads up to the climax. Expect students to discuss the rationale behind every placement. Connect the dots to create a visual plot line for the story.

Different perspectives may result in the identification of different points of climax. These are acceptable as long as they are supported. Sometimes we follow up on the most unusual choice in discussion.

For example, in Mayling's class one day, a student suggested that the climax of *Perseus and Medusa* is at the beginning of the story, when the child was born. It gradually became clear that this student was viewing the events through the eyes of the grandfather, a minor character. Mayling confirmed this novel interpretation by asking the class to help make a second plot line from this new perspective. She concluded by stressing the validity and "correctness" of all answers as long as students have good reasons to support their thinking.

Teachers who wish to revise their programs to incorporate a Whole Language view must provide daily opportunities for shared reading. Since most teachers already read to their students, this component is an easy one to start with.

We have tried to present many practical ideas in a usable form, but teachers must not simply adopt them as activities without developing their own understanding of the principles behind the implementation. The activities are not ends in themselves. The object is to stimulate students' interest, enjoyment, and understanding of reading and to build a bridge to successful independent reading. Observe your students, and then reflect on the effectiveness of your approach.

The bottom line is, are your students excited by books and stories? Do they discuss them seriously, or do they merely go through the motions and try to second-guess what the teacher expects?

INDEPENDENT WRITING

A Shift in Roles

One major change we made in our program was radically to increase the amount of writing we expected from students. Daily, as part of normal school routine, we asked them to write independently, expressing their ideas in any way they could. This new approach required that we take on a much different role ourselves. Instead of being "topic assigners" and "correctors," we became responders to authors and their communications. We all learned a great deal from this experience. Once our students found writing accessible and purposeful, they pursued it with great energy. They enjoyed their writing and we enjoyed responding to it. They became fluent, confident writers. When we stepped back and studied our students' progress, we found they were making sense of the writing system by reconstructing it.

In this chapter we describe one writing program for early primary, and another program for later primary and intermediate students. However, the programs are continuous. We are simply shifting our focus to accommodate students' maturing abilities. We also discuss key ingredients of progress: topic choice and conferencing (Graves, 1983).

Topic Selection

We want students to take control of their own writing and produce writing based on their own experiences. Encouraging students to write about everyday events validates these as topics. Therefore topic choice is at the core of the routine. We do not find that students get stuck "because they have nothing to write about." They get ideas from personal experiences at home and at school, from the books they read, from shared reading, from class discussions, and from each other.

Joy asked her primary class how they decided on their topics. These three responses were typical:

- "We just use our imaginations and write our stories."
- "We imagine . . . and sometimes we tell stuff that is true."
- "We can write real stories or things you make up."

Students write when writing serves a function for them, and when they believe their personal expression is valued. We find that regular writing conferences fulfilling these needs are essential for progress.

General Principles for Conferencing

Conferences involve authors and listeners, who exchange ideas in their discussion of a particular piece of writing. During a conference we expect an author to read his or her own writing, and we expect the audience to listen intently, attempting to form a clear image of what the author means. Listeners respond to the meaning first. Once they have that clear, they become readers who assist with details of form.

Student/teacher or student/student discussions occur prior to, during, or following a piece of writing. We demonstrate appropriate responses ourselves and initiate discussion topics such as, "How can an audience best help a writer?" We keep certain strategies in mind when we conference with young authors. First we connect with the writing in some way. We reflect the author's meaning (paraphrasing), ask questions for clarification, or contribute an idea or experience of our own.

Next we confirm good characteristics that exist in the piece, and celebrate an author's exploration of new strategies and topics. We acknowledge attributes such as the structure (sequence, categorizing, organization of information), the development (beginning, middle, end), clarity of expression, and descriptive details.

Then we extend the writing by asking the author to explain, clarify, or add more information (of meaning and structure). We ask for oral elaboration first, and then judge what changes we can expect in the writing considering the ability and attitude of the writer. For example, inserting and deleting words and phrases is one early expectation. Adding to the story at the end is another.

Give students many opportunities to listen and participate in whole class and student/teacher conferences before expecting them to engage in effective, independent conferences with their peers. They must learn to recognize the interconnecting roles of writers and readers; that is, the responsibility of writers to respond to the concerns of their readers, and the role of readers to support and extend the writing of writers.

Independent Writing Procedures: Early Primary

We expect our students to use what they know of written language to express their ideas. Of course, our youngest writers do not follow all the conventions of written English. But we ask them to express their ideas through drawing as well, thereby providing a meaningful context. Here is how we start and maintain such a program.

A. Setting

Preferred arrangement — seating in small groups with a central source of supplies.

B. Materials

Half-and-half notebooks, pencils, colored felts or crayons.

C. Initial Instructions

Draw a picture and write about it. When you are finished, come and read your writing to a teacher.

D. Procedure

1. We move about the classroom, printing the date in students' books (unless they prefer to print their own dates). We reinforce students who have started writing; for example, "Oh! You've got an idea already. Good for you!" We observe how each writer is proceeding. Once the program is established, we take care to note strategies such as: which students ask others for help, what kinds of help they request, what understand-

ings they display, what awareness or use of letter-sound correspondences they reveal.

2. Some students may ask for our help initially. However, we do not suggest topics, spell words, or otherwise take responsibility for the writing. If a student is hesitant to begin or overly concerned about his or her ability to write, we might say:
   - "It's your work. Do it any way you can."
   - "Use your own spelling. You'll be able to read it."
   - "Just begin your drawing. It will give you ideas for your writing."

3. Students approach us for a conference when they are ready. Usually several come at once and so, informally, they are able to hear each other's writing and respond to it. We ask them to read their writing to us. We observe their rereading strategies, analyze their pieces of writing, and compare these with what we have observed of their writing strategies during the writing. In this way we begin to form a profile of what they can do and how we can best help them. As listeners/readers we always respond first to the meaning. For example, we may do one of these:
   - Paraphrase the child's message.
   - Contribute some personal experience that relates to the meaning.
   - Ask a question for clarification or more information.

4. After such a response we may comment on or ask about transcription strategies; for example:
   - "Can you show me where it says _____ ?"
   - "Yes! I see an s for *sun*."
   - "Can you tell me about _____ ?" (Point to print.)

   We all celebrate new discoveries and the good thinking they represent. Informal conferences with several students set the stage for the development of effective techniques for peer conferencing.

5. We transcribe student writing that is not clearly readable onto the back page of the notebook (in the cursive form so that we do not seem to be correcting the writer). We add the date and any information regarding change in the writer's strategies. We especially note when students begin to use specific letters to represent sounds in words (semiphonetic).

6. Students move on to a quiet, prearranged activity.

Development of Transcription

We observe and analyze the strategies our young writers use to transcribe their ideas into print. Our findings (Chow, 1990; Dobson, 1989) and those of such researchers as Read (1971), Gentry (1982), and Temple, Nathan, and Burris (1982) indicate patterns in the growth of students' strategies. We describe these as five levels of development:

A. Prephonetic

This level is characterized by young children's first attempts to write, whether it be scribble writing, mock alphabetic writing (circles and lines), or alphabetic writing (series of letters). Such a writer is not operating with the understanding that letters correspond to sound units of English. As a result the writer uses the support of accompanying drawings to read and compose freely. The message and the wording are not stable but change with successive readings by the writer.

Cursive-like.

The rabbit is going to the fair.

Letter-like.

ĒILE PʰO f L C(S

"Santa Claus is coming now. I can
see his presents and I just peep in
one eye and I see Santa bring
present for me."

B. Semiphonetic

At this level young writers systematically use some letters to represent words or parts of words in their message. They use letters
such as *U* for *you* and *L* or *el* and other letter-sound correspondences as they perceive them (usually first letters in words). At
this point they tend to reduce the length and difficulty of their
compositions and focus attention on transcription. Their letter-
name strategy is unconventional in adult terms, but is systematic
and functional in terms of their existing understanding of the
writing system.

Use of letter names.

I know you.

Partial phonetic representation.

THE JJBMNR.

The Gingerbread man.

C. Phonetic

Writers at this level attempt a total mapping of the sound-letter correspondences that they perceive, using their own phonological judgment to decide on the transcription. They sound through their message as they write, organizing spellings on the basis of their place of articulation in the mouth. They use vowels in appropriate places, but the vowels used are not always the expected ones. Such writers may acknowledge word boundaries initially by placing periods, dashes, slash marks, or even colons between words! Nasals (/n/ or /m/) that occur before consonants are not recognized as a change of articulation and are, therefore, generally omitted from spellings. At this level many students begin to do some minor editing on the basis of meaning.

Jan 2;
Bernade

The: Gɑʟ: Soo: A: Gi6 ʌ ɛ Brɑd/Mon
and: D. Sʌi: Da ʌi: to ɛ at: it: For
tea.

The girl saw a gingerbread man and decided to eat it for tea.

Last night I had the best babysitter in the world.

D. Transitional

Writers' strategies change from a reliance on phonology or sound for representing words to much greater reliance on morphophonemic strategies that incorporate aspects of grammar and meaning. At this point their writing is quite readable. They continue to use a sounding-out strategy for difficult words. However, they produce a number of sight words as visual units, thus integrating visual and auditory strategies in spelling. This integration is crucial for future development.

Feb 9, 88

When I Grow up I Will be A Labrbyen helper I am going to help little kids to Find Good Books For Them.

Labrbyen = librarian

As students progress along the continuum, support newly-discovered visual strategies over lower level strategies of sounding-out.

E. Conventional

Writers now use conventional spellings automatically for a large core of commonly used words. They are working on conventions of punctuation and other matters of form. They are also able to concentrate more of their energy on matters of composition. Most children do not reach this stage in the primary grades.

Development of Composition

Children's early writings display a variety of everyday language functions (Taylor, 1983; Teale and Sulzby, 1986). They may write lists, requests, demands, and announcements. For example, when Mayling's five-year-old son couldn't attract her attention with scribble memos, he wrote the following to express his displeasure.

- URFR (You are fired.)
  Just as young children point at people and objects and name them, so our young writers often name or label items in their drawings.
- Shirley wrote: TT (tent), MN (moon).
- Sam drew and named the people important to him:
  This is my mom, this is my dad, this is my sister, this is my friend.

Such early manifestations of writing simply describe what can be seen on the page. But in some instances the caption or label represents more than just one simple word. It often stands for a sentence or even a story. Young writers, like young speakers, expect listeners/readers to fill in the gaps with the rest of the communication. They assume a context of shared meaning.

Children take a further step once they begin to tell about their own experiences. The language used retains the characteristics of "talk written down." However, the major context shifts from the drawing to the writing. We notice that most of the previous examples have this quality; for example, Last night I had the best babysitter in the world. We find that such journal pieces gradually grow in length until they include several thoughts. Our students often begin their story-writing by retelling favorite stories. First they write a sentence or two as in the following.

- JACK KnLiBON The BUNSOK BuT onthe WAY He SAE A GAYT. (Jack climbed on the beanstalk but on the way he saw a giant.)
  In time students add more details and adopt expressions and structures particular to written language. Sometimes they alter the characters, setting, and even the plot of an existing story to their own liking. They have become aware that writers control and manipulate all these aspects.

Once they become confident in both composing and transcribing, they branch out and experiment with many different styles and genres. Lia, a first grade student of Joy's, wrote the following in poetic form.

The sun is yellow
The leaves are happy
The leaves have lots of color and they swirl around you
and then shrivel up and die.

While there is a general overall progression, young writers do move back and forth between the various levels. For example, when writers are working on aspects of transcription, composition may fall back to a lower level. Don't be concerned. Always respond to the meaning and expect writers to elaborate orally. Once they assimilate their new strategies, they will apply them at a more complex level.

Independent Writing Procedures: Late Primary and Intermediate

Once students are writing longer compositions that can stand on their own without the support of drawings and are conventional enough for us to read, we suggest a change to lined paper. The timing of this change depends on the experience and maturity of the writers. However, it usually occurs near the beginning of second grade. Because we initiate longer, more formal conferences, we cannot continue to see each student every day. But we also find we don't need to. They have now become self-sustaining writers. Our procedure with later primary and intermediate students is as follows.

A. Setting

Preferred arrangement — seating to accommodate quiet communication. Arrange to have areas where students may go for uninterrupted work and for conferences.

B. Materials

• Teacher Conference Record Forms.

TEACHER CONFERENCE RECORD				
Date	Name	Title	Conference points/ priority	Future plan

- Student Conference Record Forms.

STUDENT CONFERENCE RECORD		
Title	Date Started	Conference points/Commitment

- A folder for each student's writing with record forms stapled to the inside cover.
- Lined newsprint paper.
- Foolscap paper.
- Tape and scissors.

C. *Initial Instructions*

We'll be writing on a regular schedule. I'm interested in what you have to say. You can write about anything you choose, providing it's appropriate in a classroom.

Enter today's date and the title of your first piece of writing on the record sheet. It is your responsibility to keep this sheet up to date.

Write quickly and get your ideas down any way you can. Don't worry about spelling at this time. You don't have to finish by the end of the period. You will continue tomorrow where you left off today. If you finish a piece of writing, begin another one. The rough draft paper is here. Please write on every second line (this habit takes time to establish) and on one side of the paper. You will need the extra room for editing and revisions. Get a new sheet of paper when you need it. Date all your work. Put all your writing in your folder regardless of its condition, including false starts.

D. Early Conferences

We begin to conference on the first day by walking around the class and commenting on the students' efforts. We might say:

- "What a great title! I can imagine the kinds of adventures that can happen with a title like that."
- "Great! I think you are writing one of my favorite stories. I can hardly wait to read it."
- "Still stuck for an idea? How about beginning with a picture? That might give you an idea for writing later."

At the end of a period we extend an invitation to students to read or tell the class what they have written so far. This allows for more ideas for future topics and for the rehearsing of the next day's writing. Later this sharing of writing may be restricted to a scheduled time called "Authors' Time."

When the students become comfortable with the routine and the expectations for continuous writing, we begin scheduling students into longer and more formal conferences. We listen to students reading their own writing, one at a time or in a group. Later in this chapter, we describe an actual sequence of conferences on a single piece of writing.

PRACTICAL SUGGESTIONS

1. If possible, have students write every day but, at the least, three times a week. If your time is limited, schedule periods on subsequent days to provide the continuity that is so important.
2. Periods 25 to 30 minutes long may be adequate at the beginning of the program, but expect to lengthen the time to 40 minutes. Give a 5-minute warning that the period is ending. Remind students that they will be able to continue their writing the next time.
3. If students are overly concerned about spelling, suggest they circle problem words for now and deal with them later during a conference.
4. Once the class is settled, engage in your own writing or conferencing and be unavailable to assist students. This demonstrates that you personally value literacy. You are practising what you are preaching. Don't worry if some students find it difficult to begin; they'll pick up on the example of others.

5. Briefly acknowledge the progress in students' writing before the end of the first day. Place your initials at the end of the writing to acknowledge writing done so far and to monitor the extent of future writing.
6. Use writing "jargon" whenever possible; for example, *draft; revising; editing; publishing; conferencing; beginning; middle; end; introduction; your characters; your readers*.
7. Remind students about carets and the advantages of crossing out instead of erasing. This will lead to the use of the cut and paste method. It's more important that a piece be coherent and well organized than that it look good.
8. Give short mini-lessons, pep talks, and reminders on a regular basis. Use good examples from student writing.
9. Encourage writers to come for a conference when they're stuck and to get ideas from others.
10. Post first and second draft samples on classroom bulletin boards to spread ideas and motivation.
11. Insist that students keep accurate records of dates, topics, conferences, and commitments.
12. Keep personal records indicating student progress and the strategies that need formal group instruction.

PRIORITIES AS A GUIDE TO CONFERENCING

It is difficult to come up with a blueprint for writing conferences. Each writer is unique and therefore needs to be approached differently. Nonetheless there are priorities to follow, which emphasize writers' responsibilities to readers and elements of composition that best serve fledgling writers' attempts to communicate with readers. These priorities are:

A. Meaning (Story Format)

- Elaboration (explain, clarify who/what/where/when/why/how).
- Structure (sequence, categorize, organize information).
- Development (beginning, middle, end).

B. English Grammar

- Sentence units (concept of sentence, periods).
- Sentence structure (word order, tenses, connectives, . . .).
- Punctuation (possessives, quotation marks, . . .).

C. Word Level

- Vocabulary choice, usage.
- Spelling.

The conferencing format becomes more formal as writers mature. Mature writers are not identified by age or grade, but by certain characteristics. Mature writers have:

- The ability to read and write independently.
- The ability to analyze and reflect on their own language.
- The ability to manipulate their own writing.
- An awareness of differences between speech and writing.
- An awareness of reader needs and corresponding writer responsibilities.

Once writers begin to analyze and manipulate their own writing, they are ready to focus on their composition of ideas. How each writer organizes his or her writing reflects that writer's level of maturity. Our understanding and acceptance of each writer's abilities provide the nurturing environment for a productive writing conference. However, we must first observe what our young writers are doing. Significant questions include the following.

- Does the writing reflect some recognition of an audience?
- Which students are risk-takers and willingly attempt new forms of written expression?
- Are they aware of the many styles of writing, and that different functions require different styles?
- Which writers are finding their "own voice" or writing in a way that distinctly reflects their personalities?

Young writers' conceptual awareness of the many possibilities in composition and their willingness to take risks while writing determine how we respond to them during a writing conference. Within conferences, we seek to confirm their vast knowledge of the written language and to encourage its further exploration. Only through many experiences with writing can young writers begin to induce the rules and conventions of written expression.

A SAMPLE STORY CONFERENCE

In the following example Mayling is conferencing with Donny, a young student who is learning English as a second language.

Initially Donny had an idea that may have come out of his previous work, other children's writing, life experience, or reading experience. This particular example seems to have been inspired by a familiarity with fairy tales and the Mr. Greedy series of reading books (Hargraves, 1981).

Donny drafted a version of his story and shared it with an audience — his teacher. As he read his story, he began to edit; rephrasing parts, making additions and self-correcting for spelling and punctuation. (We expect writers to come to the writing conference with a pencil in hand, and we encourage them to make necessary changes as they go.) Donny made a number of improvements to his writing before Mayling responded at all!

> Mr. Strong
> One morning Mr. Strong went out to get wood for his fireplace. He went into the forest to get the wood but he forgot to bring his axe. He said "Who care. I will use my hand." So he used his hand and chopped down lots of trees, and then he chopped them into a lot of pieces. Mr. Strong was very strong. He can build a house in just only one week. He can even lift up a four thousand years old tree. Mr. Strong was named Mr. Strong because he was very strong.
>
> _
>
> Soon after a few years Mr. Strong's house was getting old. He decided to build another house. Mr. Strong was so strong it took him to build his house just only one week. After living in his new house one of his friends came and said "You are still very strong." And then he went. When his friend went he said to himself "I will always be very strong."

The first conference focused on meaning and story format (conferencing priority A). After Donny read his story, Mayling praised its introduction and development of character. She then asked him to draw a line where his description of Mr. Strong ended (see the broken line). This exercise resulted in Donny offering to "write more" so that the storyline would be longer than the introduction. A discussion of quantity versus quality followed. Mayling then asked Donny what kind of story he had planned to write. He said it was like a fairytale. A review of the elements of a fairytale ensued. At this point Donny said he required no further conferencing since he knew exactly what he wanted to do with his story.

Second Draft

A few days later Donny came back for a second conference with a revised draft in hand. He had crossed out the section after the line and replaced it with the following.

> So one day, there was a contest of who can build the fastest house. The contest only allow two people on one team. Every team had two people but Mr. Strong was just by himself. So he can't join the contest. Then he went home. When he got home there was a man standing beside his door. He asked "Who are you?" The man answered "My name is Mr. Fast." He said, "I am named Mr. Fast because I do things very fast." Then Mr. Strong had an idea. He asked Mr. Fast to join the contest with him. Mr. Fast did and they both started being friends. When the contest day came, they were ready. Then the contest began. One of the men said "go" and they all started. Mr. Strong and Mr. Fast was the fastest team. They were working very fast. Mr. Fast was giving wood to Mr. Strong and Mr. Strong was nailing the wood very fast too. They were fast because one of them was fast and one of them was strong. It only took them two hours to finish building a house. Mr. Strong and Mr. Fast were the winners and the other teams were not even finished building their roofs. Then after one of the men gave them the trophy. Then they went home with their trophy, and Mr. Fast was living in Mr. Strong's house, and they lived happily ever after.
> The End.

The more thoroughly developed plot of the second draft now satisfies reader expectations. While retaining the theme of superhuman feats, Donny nevertheless has made some very appropriate additions and changes to his story format. He observes story conventions by setting up a problem and then provides a solution through the introduction of Mr. Fast. His conclusion conforms most satisfactorily to fairytale guidelines. As a writer Donny has competently fulfilled his responsibilities to his readers.

The second conference concerned sentence structure (part of conferencing priority B). Donny was able to combine some of his sentences and improved the grammar in others. This edited version was then proofread for spelling (part of conferencing priority C). Donny circled the words whose spelling he was unsure of, and Mayling printed the conventional spelling where necessary (ticking some that were already correct). This process requires children to make judgments concerning the conventionality of their own spelling, which is an important step in its development. Now Donny was ready to produce his final copy for publication.

Final products are part of the process of learning to write. Teachers must accept students' "final" drafts even though they still contain unconventional grammar, spelling, and punctuation.

PREPARING FOR PUBLICATION

After students have written and conferenced a number of pieces, we expect them to select one to polish for publication. At this point they must read their writing objectively, from the point of view of a reader. They may need several conferences to focus first on composition and then on details of transcription.

Writers are responsible for asking for help when and where they need it. We ask them to circle words when they are unsure of the spelling. Then we provide the conventional forms, explaining derivation when appropriate.

We treat student publication as legitimate reading material. We use good paper and feature the finished work in a prominent place.

- Respond to content before form.
- Restrict yourself to one point during each conference.
- Refrain from taking control of students' writing.

We realize that, in the past, with our external standard of correctness, we actually made writing difficult and uninteresting. Now that we allow topic choice and discuss writers' ideas seriously in a conferencing format, students find writing an easy and pleasurable experience. They also find it challenging and purposeful. Especially exciting for us is seeing students' growing competency and their pleasure in sharing writing with their peers.

Our beginning writers delight in first drawing and then writing their messages. Surprisingly they apply their knowledge of sound-letter correspondences in their writing before they do this in their reading. By writing any way they can, our students show astonishing progress in the use of writing conventions. Of all the literacy activities, it is writing that gives the most accurate and valuable diagnostic information. Thus it is writing that serves to inform and refine all our teaching.

INDEPENDENT READING

A Shift in Roles

We view reading as a language process in which readers use all their background knowledge to predict and test a re-creation of meaning. This background knowledge is multifaceted. It includes knowledge of the world, of books and book language, and of multilevel language cue systems. These cue systems consist of meaning, grammar, and graphophonics, which refers to the correspondence of patterns of sounds to patterns of letters. We view the learning process as one of successive approximations to proficient reading. Therefore we immerse our students in the full process. They learn to make sense of reading through actually reading.

Therefore we made a vital change when we increased the amount of reading we expected our students to do. Daily, as part of normal school routine, we asked them to read on their own, working at the development and integration of their reading strategies any way they could. In this situation, they read silently or aloud, relying on their own resources to get to the meaning. This approach required us to take on a much different role ourselves. Instead of assigning selections and correcting errors, we became responders to readers' interpretations. We became coaches in students' selection of materials and their use of reading strategies.

We all learned a great deal from this shift in roles. Once our students found reading accessible and purposeful, they pursued it with great energy. They enjoyed their reading and we enjoyed responding to their interpretations. They became fluent, confident readers.

In this chapter we describe one reading program for early primary, and another for later primary and intermediate students. However, the programs are continuous. We are simply shifting our focus to accommodate students' maturing abilities. We also discuss the key ingredients to progress: book selection and conferencing.

Book Selection

As in independent writing, we want our students to take control of their own learning by choosing reading material that is interesting, meaningful, and, at the same time, appropriate to their ability level. Therefore book choice is at the heart of the routine.

We find that our students respond to reading choice in different ways according to their interests and personalities. Some like to reread favorites over and over. However, we may wish they would extend their repertoires. Others choose material that is so difficult in concept and/or vocabulary that they cannot sustain the meaning. They need guidance to choose easier reading. Our goal for students is that they develop the strategies and courage to challenge themselves appropriately. Therefore we first observe their own choices and progress. Then, using our experience and judgment, we decide whether to assist, challenge, or let them be.

When in doubt, do not interfere with readers' control over their own reading.

General Principles for Conferencing

At the center of the reading conference is a conversation about a book. It may involve a group of students, or one student and a teacher. The focus is on meaning, as readers respond to the story and reflect on what the author is trying to do.

In a student/teacher conference, we first connect with the reader's interpretation. Next we confirm the logic of this response and celebrate the student's ability to provide supporting evidence. Only then do we attempt to extend the student's thinking by asking him or her to consider other possible opinions or perspectives.

The language and focus of our reading conferences are similar to those of our shared discussions. The key is to pose skilful, open-ended questions. Our most basic comprehension question for a fiction selection is one that asks students to retell the story in their own words. When they have spontaneously retold all the events they can, we assist them in drawing out the important events and forming them into a summarized plot statement. Most fiction is structured around a problem that the character or characters have to solve. We help students ask about the problem(s) in the story and how it/they were solved. We expect them to substantiate their opinions with evidence from events in the story.

We also ask them to reach further into the meaning and to consider the theme. One way of helping students detect theme is to ask what they have learned about people or life from the story. We then go on to ask how they react to this theme, or if it has some personal meaning for them (pages 20–25).

Once students provide a summarized plot statement, we go directly to questions at the deeper levels of understanding. At this point it would be patronizing to ask literal questions about events. We do not ask questions to "test" knowledge, but to extend reading and thinking strategies. The major purpose of discussing stories is to develop a reflective stance towards reading and to validate personal interpretation.

We have drawn up a list of open-ended questions that provide alternate routes to reaching the deeper understanding that our students often have but do not realize they have, or would not think of volunteering without our further probing. We model these extensively in class discussions of our shared reading. Our students gradually internalize the questions that we ask, coming to ask these questions themselves. They then have these strategies available to apply to their independent reading.

Following are examples of open-ended questions concerning stories.

A. *Characters*

- What characters were in the story?
- Tell me more about _____ .
- What other characters were there?
- Did the characters act as you expected?
- What character would you like as a friend? Why?
- Does _____ remind you of a character in another story, or of someone you know?

48

B. Events

- Tell me what happened in the story.
- You said ____ happened. Tell me more about that.
- When ____ did that, what did you think would happen?

C. Plot

- What problem (or trouble) was there in the story?
- What problem were the characters trying to solve?
- Were you worried about any of the characters? Why?
- What other story is similar to this one? How?
- Was everyone happy, or OK?

D. Theme

- What main thing was the story (or author) telling you?
- What deep truth is there in the story?
- Did anyone in the story learn anything? What? Who?
- What can we all learn from this story?
- Are there good/bad guys? Who are they?
- What good/bad things happened, or did ____ do?
- Would ____ do something different another time?
- Would you do what ____ did? Why or why not?

E. Other

Following are examples of questions for elaboration/clarification/ development of critical thinking.

- Tell me about ____ .
- You said ____ . What in the story made you think that?
- How did you know ____ ?
- What were you thinking when ____ ?
- What did you mean when ____ ?
- Were you wondering about anything?
- What questions would you like to ask the author?
- How did ____ make you feel or react?
- What part of the story did you like best? Why?
- Did anything in the story surprise you? What?

●

If students have trouble with comprehension, check for the reason. If they have difficulty even remembering or relating the events of a story, we need to examine in greater detail the strategies they use during reading.

Coaching Strategies

Whenever we listen to students reading, we are in a position to observe what they are doing. Our goal is to guide students by recognizing and confirming positive aspects of their existing strategies, and coaching them to develop their strategies in a balanced way.

We expect our students to think constantly about what they are reading, using their background knowledge to predict what will happen. As the story unfolds, we expect them to confirm or disconfirm their hypotheses. As they read, they should ask themselves such questions as:

- Does it make sense?
- Does it sound right?

Once they realize the reading doesn't make sense, we expect them to self-correct.

When readers meet an unfamiliar word, they should use the context, including illustrations, to predict what it might be. They may have to reread or read past the immediate text to get more context. They may have to ask themselves, "What will make sense and sound right?" Once students have produced an approximation that works, they can apply their knowledge of phonics, especially to the initial letters in words, and compare their prediction with the text.

Vicki, a second grade student, was reading aloud from *Little Red Hen* (Melser, 1980). Marietta observed that Vicki hesitated for a long time before correctly reading *milk* in the following sentence. Then she shouted out the word in a triumphant voice.

- Who will get me some . . . milk for the cake?

In a post-reading conference with Marietta, the following conversation took place:

M. = Marietta.   V. = Vicki.

M. Vicki, did you have any problems in your reading?
V. Yes, I didn't know this word (indicating *milk*).
M. So what did you do?
V. I sounded it.
M. Yes, that can help. But I also noticed that you had another good idea. You looked at the picture. What did you see there?
V. I saw the milk, and I thought about m-i-l-k and said *milk*.

50

M. So you used that good idea and I could tell by your voice that you knew it made sense. Good thinking! So what can help you sometimes when you're stuck?

V. I can look at the picture.

M. Right! And then think what makes sense.

In the classroom we have neither the time nor the need to examine the reading of all our students in the detail described in the miscue analysis (pages 89–93). However, by observing and examining reading in such a qualitative way, we come to appreciate the amazing feats that our young readers are accomplishing We observe that they are progressing along a path of successive approximations to proficient reading and are using that same process. We come to realize that we can use this framework as a foundation for tapping into the reading profiles of our students and for coaching them from the sidelines. Without taking away control, we can give them positive feedback on the promising strategies they are developing, and help them bring these strategies into conscious play.

Give readers lots of time to process information. Teachers who "bite their tongues" will find this waiting time a significant factor in students' developing competencies.

Independent Reading Procedures: Early Primary

READING MATERIAL

1. A well-stocked classroom library (consisting of trade books and a variety of readers), which includes books introduced in shared reading.
2. Signs, labels, and messages naming objects, pictures, and activities in the classroom.
3. Chalkboard messages and chart board stories developed in shared writing.
4. Students' independent writing (described in chapter four).

GETTING STARTED

Learning to read can be an exciting adventure for every child. As teachers of beginning readers, we need to provide a nurturing environment that bridges the child's transition from home to school. An understanding of the reading process and of how children learn it helps us create a classroom atmosphere in which we value and respect children's early approximations to reading. We find that children develop more quickly when we accept their errors as a normal part of learning, and thereby encourage them to take risks. This is how young children acquire language at home, and how they can learn to read in the classroom.

Some children enter school with a reading vocabulary, while others barely recognize their own printed names. We want to be aware of these individual differences, so that we can challenge all our students. However, in order to accomplish this goal, we do not need to segregate students into homogeneous groups. Rather we propose open-ended activities and questions that all students can participate in successfully at their own levels. Each child is a unique individual who is moving along his or her own continuum of literacy learning.

Young readers need to know certain things in order to learn to read. They also need our support and guidance in their attempts to apply that knowledge. The following are key components of our beginning reading program. We introduce some of these activities together, and others at a later time. However, we also circle around and come back to previous activities at a higher level — in a continuous, upward spiral of learning.

PLAY-READING

We expect our students to construct meaning from books and stories even though they do not yet read conventional print. We treat this play-reading as an important activity. Students may at first rely on the illustrations and their memory of events and wordings of favorite stories to reenact the experience. This points out the value of encouraging them to choose books that we have shared previously, and to work on rereading these independently. They need time and encouragement to explore and experiment with their increasingly sophisticated understanding of the process.

Therefore we timetable periods in which all our students choose books to read to themselves in any way they can. We see them progressing through various approximations of reading, forming and testing their hypotheses as they proceed. This gives us a prime opportunity to connect with what they are trying to do. We confirm their efforts as significant and their strategies as fruitful. We extend their strategies to a conscious level and coach their use.

In this way we achieve the joint purposes of helping students see themselves as readers, and of helping them evaluate their own progress.

NAMES OF ALPHABET LETTERS

Naming is an early strategy, common to all language learners. Knowing the name of a person or object makes it seem familiar and friendly. These are feelings we wish to foster. Children need to know letter names in order to create their own spellings. (They initially use a semiphonetic letter-naming strategy, representing sounds in print by relating them to the letter-names they know, page 31.) Therefore we constantly refer to letters by name and give children many opportunities to practise their identification through games, songs, and books.

EARLY VOCABULARY WORDS

Signs and Labels

We live in a print-filled environment that surrounds children with written language in such forms as directions and advertising long before they enter school. In fact, the beginnings of reading development often go unnoticed, with neither children nor parents aware that reading has begun (Y. Goodman, 1980). We consciously create situations so that our beginning readers can demonstrate and apply what they already know. Signs in the environment provide excellent reading material for beginning readers. We are usually pleasantly surprised to discover the extent of students' knowledge when we focus on what they "can do."

We take our students on a walk around the school to identify signs such as EXIT, BOYS, OFFICE, using the environmental context as a guide to identification. We ask, "How do you know?" This makes their strategies explicit and available for use (Dobson and Hurst, 1982). And so, right from the beginning, our students develop a functional literacy. Following the walk through the school or community, we bring replicas such as photographs or posters into the classroom, displaying them on a bulletin board as reminders and for reading practice.

Names

Names are significant words for young children. They often learn to read their own names and those of family members before they attend school. Joy Nucich extends this learning to include classmates' names. Her technique is to hold up student exercise books, one by one. The objective is that the students recognize the name, and the owner can claim the exercise book. The repetition of this routine exposes students to classmates' names in a meaningful way. They eventually take over this activity, eagerly reading names and distributing sets of books. This genuine task enables students to learn a great deal about each other.

Literacy learning is not a solitary activity but a social one. It is interesting to watch Joy's young students help each other handing out books. When her kindergarten and first grade students confuse names such as Paul, Parminder, and Peter, she knows they are using first letters as an identifying feature. When she observes children formulating rules about letter-sound correspondences, she knows they will be able to benefit from phonics instruction and beginning activities in a reader. Every few weeks she records the names children can identify, thus documenting their progress.

Word Cards

We print the words students recognize at sight on word cards. These words become their first reading vocabulary. At the beginning of each day, each student chooses a key word and illustrates it in a small *Very Own Word* booklet. We print the word on a small card as well (old library cards work well). Students keep their words in envelopes labeled *My Words*.

Once students know about five key words, we begin to work them into sentences. With the students clustered in a small group on the carpet, we print a sentence on the chalkboard, and they manipulate their cards to reproduce it. This activity engages students in using conventions of print such as directionality and word separation. We have students read their sentence, pointing to each word in turn. Once they can do this easily, we encourage them to create their own sentences, reading them to themselves, peers, and teachers.

Most children treasure their word cards and enthusiastically ask for new words, including verbs and articles, so that they can make new sentence constructions. In this way they learn function words in a meaningful context. For example, we print *Come to the KINDER-GARTEN* and ask students to identify and carry out the instruction. This allows us to keep the central focus squarely on meaning. If students do not remember certain words, we eliminate these words from their collections. We do the same with other variations such as *Come to the* BOYS' *washroom* and *Come to see the* GIRLS *and* BOYS. (Sight words appear in upper case letters as they do in their original environmental context.)

Within this routine we talk about our strategies, using the language and vocabulary of conventional literacy (*letter, word, sentence, period, question mark*). We ask, "How did you know that?" We are laying the groundwork for students to understand the concepts of written language.

Once students have approximately 30 words in their envelopes, the stack of cards becomes unmanageable. At this point children no longer seem to need to manipulate the word cards physically, so they take them home and move on to other activities.

We also write sentences on the chalkboard, using words students are familiar with. To begin, a group reads the sentence together and practises following the print from left to right and top to bottom. All the students join in, each at his or her own level. In the meantime, students are also learning to read names of classmates, colors, and objects labeled in the classroom. They do this without direct instruction and the resulting knowledge enables them to formulate connections between letters and sounds, which they use to "read" unfamiliar print.

October 15 — One Student's Word Cards

house
OFFICE
run

rainbow
KINDERGARTEN
jump

tree
BOYS
is

apple
GIRLS
to

car
Mother
the

Lisa
Father
up

Mrs. Nucich
GO
a

EXIT
see
down

STOP
look
I

MACDONALD'S
can
. (period)

Examples of Core Vocabulary Sentences

- Go to the EXIT.
- Come and see Mrs. Nucich.
- KINDERGARTEN girls can jump.
- Run and STOP at the OFFICE.
- Look at the red apple.

PHONICS

We closely observe our students' independent writing to record their first instances of mapping sounds by specific letters. We encourage them to use their knowledge to reread their writing also. Once they can sustain this strategy, we know it is time to consolidate their knowledge of conventional phonic connections.

We begin with the consonants. Later, when vowels appear in students' writing, we introduce vowels. There is no need to drill or assign worksheet pages. We focus on the sound of one letter by simply brainstorming and drawing pictures of the word on the board. The students use crayons to create a composite picture of appropriate words the following day (as in Kelley's example). This simple way of teaching phonics is very effective when combined with independent writing. Our students learn to connect sounds and letters because they are using them daily to communicate their messages.

BEGINNING TO READ BOOKS: SELF-SELECTED

We set aside time at least twice a day for students to choose their own books for reading. At this time we expect them to select and read favorite storybooks independently, any way they can. Some students continue to play-read, but other students, who have developed a sight vocabulary and reading strategies, begin tracking the print. Then we may help them choose books at their level of ability. However, we do not force the issue. They learn to select reading material only when they feel free to take risks and have many varied experiences with books.

This "noisy" reading time may be called USSR (Uninterrupted Sustained Silent Reading), SQUIRT (Sustained, Quiet, Uninterrupted, 'Reading,' Time) or SSR (Sustained Silent Reading). Even though the *S* in the acronyms suggests a silent time, we know that young readers need to hear themselves reading. Therefore we not only allow but insist on students' reading aloud. As they read, we listen in to note and coach strategies in use. Early in the year we establish routines for selecting books and putting them away.

LITERACY PLAY

Literacy play activities happen whenever students are free to choose their own books and activities. Joy plans this kind of choosing activity for a 40-minute period at least three times a week. Her observations of students during this time show that they often repeat classroom activities, taking on the roles of student and teacher. Individually or in groups, the children play school, sing songs, read enlarged texts on the floor or on chart stands, read *Big Books* and small books (to and with each other), and write notes and letters. Thus they reenact reading instruction, explore and experiment with their developing understanding, and learn from each other. We find such literacy play occurs naturally when reading and writing are valued aspects of the classroom environment.

Literacy Play Observed and Overheard

1. One student says to another, "Just play read — that's what I do."
2. Two girls, using the illustrations of *The Three Little Kittens* to "read," disagree on the story so each gives her own version before they continue.
3. Three girls chant a rhyme from *Sounds I Remember* (Martin, 1972) and then make up their own version.
4. One boy walks around proudly holding a book under his arm. He approaches a group of four children and asks the best reader in the group for help.
5. Two boys sing a song from an enlarged text. One leads like a teacher and the other does the copycat part.

BEGINNING TO READ BOOKS: TEACHER-SELECTED

Beginning readers also need the guidance and expertise of their teachers to maximize their progress. One secret is supplying the right material at the right time. We have a responsibility to intelligently observe students' development and select reading materials appropriately. We discussed the importance of "quality" reading books in the shared reading section (page 36). However, beginning readers have a special need for "easy reading" books. We use selected books from the *Story Box* series (Melser, 1980), the Dobson and Hurst (1982) "sign" books, *Tiger Cub Books* (McCracken, 1989) and other beginning readers. Joy has had great success with the old reader *Off to School* (Copp Clark, 1960). We prefer to use several readers from different series, so that students experience a variety of writing styles and material. We look for stories they enjoy and language that is natural and predictable.

We hear our beginning readers read individually or in pairs, so we can coach their strategies and monitor their growth. When they encounter a new vocabulary word, we encourage them to use the context of the story to figure it out independently. We allow them a lot of time to do so. We don't worry about sensible predictions that don't exactly match the text; for example, *Daddy* for *father*. Our readers are also free to ask for help. We say, "What would make sense here? What clues do you have?" When we consistently expect readers to think for themselves, we find fluent reading comes quickly. Readers soon enjoy the challenge of stories by authors such as Robert Munsch; for example, *Paper Bag Princess*, 1980, and collections of fairytales and folktales such as those distributed by Troll Associates.

NON-FICTION READING

Students are hungry to learn about the world. Many new non-fiction materials are being published so there is a need to select materials carefully and try out a variety of presentations. Young students in Joy's class enjoy reading about endangered species in the *MacDonald Series* (1989) within an ecology theme. Students connect well with the information in the *Child's First Library and Learning Series* (Time-Life, 1989) because of its familiar question-answer format.

We also introduce knowledge through shared reading and discussion. The class composes group experience stories, which then become available for independent reading. The content material of social studies and science usually forms the basis for themes that are integrated across the curriculum.

Independent Reading Procedures: Late Primary and Intermediate

SETTING

Seating to accommodate quiet communication is the preferred arrangement. Set up a place where students may go for uninterrupted work, and a conversation area for shared reading and peer conferencing.

MATERIALS

- Teacher Conference Record forms (also used in independent writing conferences: page 37).

- Student Conference Record forms (independent writing: page 38).
- A fully lined exercise book.
- Envelopes to hold exercise books.
- Individual student folders with record forms stapled to one inside cover and envelopes to the other.

BOOKS

We select a large number and variety of illustrated fiction and non-fiction books at varying levels of complexity on the basis of quality, variety, and interest. The books represent exposure to a greater variety of authors and genres and to a greater range of language complexity than students would probably choose for themselves. We include reading selections introduced in shared reading because they tend to become favorites and because our less mature readers, particularly, need familiar stories to support their weaker reading strategies. We also provide copies of basal readers from which students can choose individual stories.

INITIAL INSTRUCTIONS TO STUDENTS

We'll be reading on a regular schedule. Reading time will follow writing time. For the first little while, we will switch to reading when the period bell goes. Later you can be the one to decide when you're ready to switch over. What we are working towards is a balance between reading and writing over the period of a week. You will be learning to organize yourself and your time to make sure you get this balance.

You may choose any book you wish. I'm interested in which books you like to read. Remember to open the book and read a little from somewhere in the beginning, the middle, and the end to make sure the book you choose is what you want. You may still find later that you are having difficulty making sense of your choice or that it doesn't really interest you. That's your signal that you should put the book back and choose another. You are learning how to make good choices for yourselves.

After you have finished your book, enter the date and title on your record sheet. Leave a space in case you or I want to make a comment. At the end of the line, please rate your book. If the book was easy for you to read, write the letter E; if just right, the letter R; and if a little bit challenging, a C. Remember, however, that if the book is so challenging that you can't make sense of it, you should put it back. What you want is a balance of the three.

When you finish a book, begin another one. For longer books, you don't have to finish by the end of the period. You will continue tomorrow where you left off today.

READING RESPONSE JOURNALS

We suggest leaving these until students are ready to begin working in them independently. For some classes, this will happen by the end of October; for others, it may be February or March. It depends on how well students respond to shared reading sessions, how well they are able to articulate their reactions to books as a group during shared writing, and how many different options we have made available regarding ways of responding to literature. When we begin the use of reading journals, we instruct students as follows.

I am interested in your individual responses to the books you have chosen. So I want you to write to me about your reactions. Think of the different ways we have talked about books. You can consider mentioning story problems and solutions, or the lessons. You may want to use a rating scale or discuss the new facts you have learned. There is no one "right" answer or response. Anything you have to say is "right" as long as you can support your statements.

You will need to make at least one entry in your reading journal each week. Sometimes I will write comments or ask questions to clarify something. I would like your response to these also. Later you may choose to share your written comments with a friend and have your friend respond to your comments in writing.

EXAMPLES FROM STUDENTS' READING RESPONSE JOURNALS

A. *Fox's Dream* (Tejima, 1987)

Student-to-teacher response

Dear Ms. Chow,

In *Fox's Dream* I couldn't really find a story problem or a solution and I could only dimly see a lesson. The book, though, made me feel very weird. It was a slow book with not many words on each page, but it made me feel nauseous and calm at the same time. It tells how a fox is walking lonely in the dark woods. Then he sees a big block of ice with many pictures in it. One picture he sees is a picture of himself and his family. Then he met another fox and they walked on. Soon it would be spring. It sort of reminded me about the times I was lonely and I was in another world.

From Wes

Teacher-to-student response

Dear Wes,

This book always gets mixed reviews. People either like it or hate it. I guess when you can relate a story the way you did, then it's pretty special. Thanks for sharing your thoughts.

Ms. Chow

B. *Comets* (F.M. Branley, 1984)

Student-to-teacher response to non-fiction

Dear Ms. Chow,

Comets is a non-fiction book that, of course, tells you about comets. I always thought that a comet had a tail because it was going fast. But I learned that a tail is formed because the tail is really dust from the comet. I also learned that, when a comet goes near the sun, the sun's gravity pulls off some of the dust and, after awhile, the comet disappears.

From Rita

C. *Loudmouth George and the Sixth-Grade Bully* (Nancy Carlson, 1985)

Student-to-student response
(Danny is a student for whom English is a second language. Both Dusty and Danny are in fourth grade.)

Hi Dusty,

I like the story *Loudmouth George and the Sixth-Grade Bully*. I like the part that when they had a plan that will trick Big Mike and I really like the part when they put tunafish sandwiches and the poured garlic powder. Danny

To Danny,

How many times did you read *Loudmouth George and the Sixth-Grade Bully*? Dusty

To Dusty,

I read it two times. Danny

To Danny,

I've read *Loudmouth George and the Sixth-Grade Bully* one time and it was good! But don't remember what it was about. Can you tell me what it's about? Dusty

Dear Dusty,

I will tell you what it is about. It's about a bunny and a bully. George the bunny was happy to go in the first day of school. And when George the bunny was going to school, suddenly a bully came up and the bully's name is Mike. He always take George's lunch away so George can pass the sidewalk but he can't because the bully is not letting George pass. I can't tell you them all. Maybe sometime. Danny

To Danny,

Let's stop writing each other! Dusty

To Dusty,

Why!!!!!!!! I don't want to!!!!!!! Danny

To Danny,

BECAUSE I WANT TO READ!!!!!!!!!!! Dusty

D. *Looking at the Body* (David Suzuki with Barbara Hehner, 1987)
Student-to-teacher response to non-fiction

Dear Ms. Chow,

New facts: Oxygen is used for burning up nutrients to make energy. You can survive a few weeks without food, a few days without water, but only a few minutes without oxygen.

Good job explaining: He did a good job explaining about the trachea (windpipe). Also about the part that you should not talk when you eat.

Confusing: The confusing part was about the diaphragm. How does the diaphragm makes the lungs bigger when the diaphragm pulls down?

From Tammy

READING CONFERENCES

We begin "spot" conferences from the very beginning. We randomly walk around the classroom asking, "How's it going?" or commenting, "Oh, that's a favorite of mine. Tell me what you think of it when you're through." Often students are reading books that we have not read. We then may comment, "What a catchy title! I don't know this book. Please come and tell me about it after you're through."

When students have settled into a routine, we begin scheduling longer and more formal conferences. Our first and most useful request is: "Tell me about this story." If we wish students to expand on their answers, we use a discussion lead such as those previously listed.

We may also check for reading strategies by asking the student to orally read specific sections of the story. This is not a threatening request when we provide a supportive environment, actively listen, and give positive feedback.

Practical Suggestions:
1. Schedule time for independent reading every day. If this time follows independent writing, then there will be a natural flow from one to the other based on individual needs and preferences.
2. Children are responsible for choosing books and settling down to read. Teachers engage in their own reading or conferences, and are unavailable for assistance.
3. Readers are responsible for the accurate recording of dates, titles, and comments on their reading selections.
4. Give short mini-lessons, pep talks, and reminders about reading strategies, levels of meaning, book choices, and routines.
5. Conduct regular conferences concerning meaning and strategies during and after reading, individually and in groups.

6. Make sure strategies and responses have been introduced and modeled in shared reading sessions (chapter three).
7. Don't expect to be able to conference with students about every book they read. Once they know the routine and understand the kinds of questions readers need to ask, they participate in group and peer conferences. In addition, we wouldn't want to limit their independent reading to the amount we can conference. Our goal is for students to choose to read for their own pleasure, and we firmly believe they learn a great deal by reading independently.
8. Develop a wide-ranging classroom collection of literature that includes novels, short stories, illustrated books, plays, letters, biographies, non-fiction, newspaper articles, magazines, readers' theater scripts, series books, essays, poetry, anthologies or basal readers, and so forth. Include the books introduced in shared reading sessions.
9. Display books in ways that encourage browsing and that focus on special interests; for example, authors, illustrators, themes, genres, reading levels.
10. Direct students to certain baskets of books if they require assistance in making better book selections. But be sparing in any grouping of books by reading level.
11. Handle basal readers in much the same way as you handle trade books. The students peruse the reader, looking for stories that interest them.
12. One day of the week may be set aside for magazines and comics that students often bring to school.

We have structured our independent reading program to enable our students to see themselves as readers in control of the process for their own purposes. To achieve this, we make their literary heritage available by immersing them in literature.

We must also support and facilitate students' reading strategies so that they have independent competency. However, in doing so, we must be careful not to focus too much on the mechanical aspects of reading, or we will risk distorting its very nature. Thus we take care to coach independent strategies within the whole process, with meaning as the central focus.

Our primary and overriding goals are to help students develop a love for literature and to provide them with independent access to it. The bottom line is, are our students choosing to read in their own time?

SHARED WRITING

A Variety of Experiences and Activities

The purpose of shared writing is to immerse students, easily and naturally, in many and varied writing experiences and to demonstrate writing in use. In a sense, shared writing encompasses all four components of the organizational framework. Any time there is writing, there must also be reading. Therefore shared writing always demonstrates shared reading. The strategies we use to transcribe and/or compose our own or students' messages demonstrate both independent writing and independent reading. The following activities highlight connections among the four components and emphasize the different ways these connections are made.

Some activities are initiated by us, and others by students. At all times, we collaborate with students to create meaningful messages. However, we are the ones who determine the particular purpose of the shared writing activity (for example, teaching reading strategies or modeling expository writing), and choose accordingly. Through shared writing, we make writing accessible to students and invite them to compose and transcribe meaning into print. In all cases we are demonstrating that writing, just like reading, involves working at all levels of language at once: meaning, grammar, and word levels.

Chalkboard Message: Early Primary

Every morning Joy Nucich prints a daily news message that could involve anything from a loose tooth to a world event. In the following example, the topic is one of universal interest — the weather!

Joy uses this chalkboard story to demonstrate the process of writing and to provide reading material. The underlying meaning is always of first importance and receives the top priority. However, she also considers structure, grammar, and wording. She selects her material to suit the maturity of her students, but also to reflect the reality of written language.

Here is Joy's chalkboard message about the weather.

It did not snow last night
The temperature is 3° outside.
Maybe it will snow today.
Yesterday we all made
snowflakes. Today we will make
them into snowpeople.

At the beginning of the school year, Joy introduces literacy terms such as *sentences, words,* and *letters* by engaging students in activities that demonstrate the underlying concepts. She asks, "How many words are in this sentence? How many letters are in this long word?" She takes advantage of students' spontaneous observations, which lead to discussions of topics such as periods, questions marks, and capital letters — what they look like, where they are used, and why.

Joy tries to be as clear as possible in her use of terms. She tries to avoid misleading practices. For example, the reality of sentences is that one sentence does not always correspond to one line of print (although primary texts are often laid out that way). When Joy wrote the accompanying example, she carefully carried one sentence on to the line below so that the punctuation mark appears in the middle, and a new sentence finishes off the line.

At times she pauses during the writing and invites students to help create the composition. One technique is to encourage students to think what will make sense and predict the next word she will print. Another technique is to use a cloze procedure in which dashes stand for the omitted words. Sometimes she prints only the first letter of the word, thereby encouraging students to use their knowledge of phonics to confirm or disconfirm their predictions. We hope students will learn such strategies through group practice so that the strategies are available when, as independent readers, students have to deal with unfamiliar words in text. We introduce the strategies in different situations, regularly, throughout the school year.

Joy uses the chalkboard message as a springboard to introduce and discuss new vocabulary and concepts including compound words, root words, prefixes and suffixes, and contractions. Each student participates at his or her own level and absorbs what s/he can from the demonstration and discussion. The more advanced Joy's students are, the more complex her message.

The easily erasable chalkboard is ideal for manipulating written language and demonstrating its flexibility. It is an opportunity for students to see teachers make mistakes (usually unintentional) and to help with corrections by checking spellings in a dictionary, using carets and other proofreading symbols, adding information, and rewriting sections for greater clarity. Young students who are interested and involved in predicting details of composition and transcription are gradually developing strategies they will use to write and read independently.

Chalkboard Message: Late Primary and Intermediate

Mayling Chow also begins her day by writing a purposeful message to her class in cursive script. The length varies, depending on variables of time, news interest, and the potential to highlight specific aspects of form. Her students read, predict, and help with punctuation and spelling as she writes. Then Mayling has the whole class reread for fluency and intonation, which means they also practise reading cursive script.

Here is Mayling's chalkboard message about the weather and events of the day.

> Can you believe the weather? Did you hear
> the thunderstorm last night? This must be what
> people mean when they say, "It's raining
> cats and dogs." How do you suppose that
> expression came about?
> Let's not forget our business for today.
> We need to get our list of nominees in by
> noon. Tomorrow we'll hear from those people
> who were nominated. At 3:00 p.m. I'd like to meet with
> all of you who agreed to be nominated.

Mayling uses the writing of the chalkboard message as an opportunity to teach formally what she discusses informally during reading and writing conferences. Initially she highlights and reinforces effective reading strategies by hesitating as she writes and encouraging students to predict her next words. Then she asks students what clues they used to make their predictions and what they can do if their predictions are disconfirmed. As Mayling's students become more adept, she shifts the focus to writing strategies. Writing done so quickly and on the spot often needs to be reworked, and this need becomes apparent to students. Mayling encourages them to suggest changes (supported by reasons) and introduces writers' "tricks of the trade" such as carets and crossouts in lieu of erasures.

The fact that students are making corrections on a teacher's work makes this activity effective yet non-threatening. It also illustrates how imperfect first drafts generally are. After the whole message has been written, reworked, and reread, Mayling directs students' attention to specifics of form such as word analysis, spelling, and language usage. For example, they may discuss root words such as *nominate* in the foregoing message, adding suffixes to make *nomination, nominated, nominee.* They may identify contractions, compound words, or homophones. The usual routine is to circle the identified words in the message and brainstorm for extensions.

Students become increasingly fascinated by the history of the English language through looking at word formation, origins, and derivations. By the time they reach the upper intermediate grades, they are ready to pursue a more in-depth study of these aspects. Mayling also introduces idiomatic expressions such as "raining cats and dogs." Students guess at the meaning and then discuss it. They look for other examples in daily conversation and in their reading, and find ways of using them.

Mayling uses the classwork engendered by the daily message as a basis for spelling lists and quizzes. For example, the morning message might have several words that end with a /ch/ sound. Students would identify these and then add more examples to the list. Mayling writes these words on the chalkboard, placing them according to spelling pattern. In this case there are two spelling groups: *coach, which, such, rich, each*; and *catch, witch, scratch, notch.* She asks students to formulate a spelling rule that will explain the groupings of the words. They might suggest that, when the spelling is *tch*, there is a "short vowel" sound preceding it. This rule is consistent. However, while some words with the *ch* spelling do not have "short vowel" sounds, a few do (*rich, which, such, much*). She then acknowledges and segregates these into a third list. The students then copy the different categories of words in their spelling books, adding more if time and space permit. Later, Mayling may arrange to have her class look more closely at "double vowels" in words such as *coach, each*. At the end of the week, Mayling and her students decide which words will form the basis of the next spelling quiz. The purpose is to ensure success for all, while at the same time challenging the most able. Therefore students choose the words they will study, and she offers bonus words or sentences for those who wish an extra challenge. Her point is not to have students memorize spellings, but to pay attention to word patterns, become curious and knowledgeable about their origins, and enjoy their study.

When you encounter students who need far more support than the rest of the class, adjust your expectations. One option is to provide the spelling of a word that students can use to work out others of the same pattern. For example, *night* may be used as the model for *right, bright*, and *knight*.

Language Experience

Groups of students, or teachers and students, cooperatively compose and transcribe meaning into text. Such transcriptions often serve as records of shared experiences such as field trips and special days. Usually the students compose and the teacher acts as scribe. Using students' own language highlights the stability of the wording of a message and the value we place on students' communications as spoken. It also makes the writing more accessible for future independent reading. We often pause as we transcribe and ask for help in that area as well.

Language experience stories are usually printed on charts or on the chalkboard. Joy and her early primary students wrote the following example.

Multicultural Day

On Friday, January 26, we celebrated Multicultural Day at Henry Hudson school. Liang's mother told us all about Malaysia. We learned many interesting things about school and living in a hot country. She made us a special dessert out of seaweed and tropical fruits. We celebrated Chinese New Year when Mrs. Nucich gave us fortune cookies. Just before lunch the whole school got a special treat of Revels because our gold brick wall is so high. In the afternoon we all watched a movie. Then Vanessa's mom came to tell us about Peru in South America. Vanessa wore a costume from Peru and we all danced to Spanish music. We had fun all day long!

Joy's class of first grade students practise their printing through the use of language experience sentences. Students have half-plain and half-lined exercise books, which they use for printing practice. They tell Joy what they want to print that day and she prints it into the book. Her students copy the sentence three times and illustrate it. She finds that students learn to print faster and better when they have ownership and interest in what they are printing. This printing book is separate from their writing exercise book, in which they both compose and transcribe their own messages.

The older students in Mayling's class collaboratively write up experiences or create stories in specific genres (fairytale, adventure, mystery). For example, one of her language groups decided to write a fairytale together. As a result of many shared reading experiences with different fairytales (classic, contemporary, and versions from other cultures), the students were able to identify elements commonly found in fairytales. They were also able to generalize kinds of story structures and language that are characteristic of fairytales. They found that fairytales usually:

- Begin with "Once upon a time" or a variation thereof.
- Happen a long time ago in a faraway land.
- Have two or three protagonists (some good, some bad).
- Result in good triumphing over evil.
- Involve magic or trickery.
- Use numbers 3 and 7 (for example, events happen in 3's).
- End with "happily ever after."

Mayling and the group collaboratively decided on setting, characters, story problem/solution (plot), and ending. Then the students composed the tale and she acted as scribe. Because her students are older, they are better able to help each other in a sensitive way to reword or rephrase original thoughts to make the written text as clear and concise as possible. At the same time, she makes every effort to honor the language abilities of all students.

●

Do not "model" writing in genres until all students are writing independently. Allow students maximum opportunities to explore different kinds of writing for themselves. In doing so, they are developing their "own voices" as writers.

Research Projects: Early Primary

Shared writing allows us to introduce research topics in content areas at an early age. We introduce topics by considering *What We Know* and *What We Want To Find Out*. When Joy asked her first and second grade students what they wanted to learn from a space unit, their list included just about everything a teacher could want or hope to teach. The abbreviated list that follows was part of a chart paper that listed everyone's ideas. A different student contributed each item. The list suggests both the depth and breadth of students' interest and curiosity about the universe.

What We Want to Learn About Space
1. Is there another solar system?
2. I want to learn more about the moon.
3. I want to learn what is on each planet.
4. What are the stars like?
5. Learn about comets.
6. Are there people on other planets?
7. Does the sun look the same from outer space?

The students went to the library where, with the help of the librarian, they located information in books and audiovisual materials. They discussed their findings and what they meant. Joy often asks her students to draw or write their findings in any way they can (as they do in independent writing). However, in this case she had them read their original questions and attempt complete answers. At the end of the exercise, her students were satisfied that they had found out what they wanted to know about space. When our younger students have been through the procedure quite a few times as a shared project, they begin to research topics on their own. The topic *Animals* makes a good introduction to personal research because it is relatively easy to organize around the simple framework of appearance, habitat, and life cycle.

Students need to have many whole class experiences with research before they are asked to gather factual information for individual projects. They need to work through the following steps with their teacher several times so that they come to understand the procedure.

1. Brainstorm *What We Know* (star information that needs to be confirmed).
2. Check outside sources for more information (by reading, viewing, interviewing, or other means).
3. Brainstorm again to add newly acquired facts.
4. Record these facts on a chalkboard or chart in some sort of visual schema such as a web or columns. Then sort the information into category groupings.
5. Decide which categories will be included in the final report, and decide on their sequence.
6. Write the first draft. In some cases we do all the writing collaboratively, taking turns composing and transcribing.
   We would not expect our younger writers to pursue report writing beyond this step. We would let our older writers write their first draft independently to encourage them to develop their own style and voice, and then hold individual student/ teacher conferences as in steps 7 and 8.
7. Conference the writing for meaning. We make sure students can articulate their understanding of the subject matter orally before we pay attention to how they express it in written form. Then we expect revisions. Several conferences may be necessary before students begin the next step.
8. Make the final editorial changes and proofread in preparation for group presentation and publication.

Research Projects: Late Primary and Intermediate

Older students usually deal with more complex topics. Therefore they continue to require many group brainstorming and teacher-directed factfinding sessions. Students who have misunderstood or who lack some basic facts are invited to work together as a group for further research and brainstorming sessions. Once students have become competent in handling steps 1 to 4 above, we encourage them to tackle more. At this stage, after we have recorded known and new information on the chalkboard, we

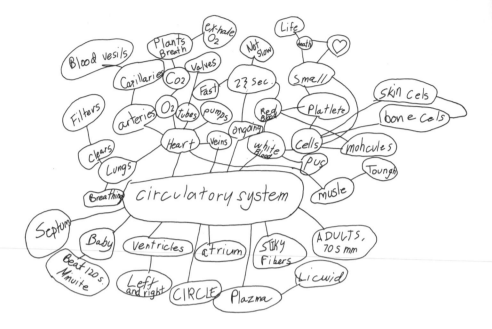

erase the results and ask students to brainstorm again, independently. We do this because we want them to write only about facts and information that are meaningful to them.

We make picture cards, hands-on kits, and audiovisual aids readily accessible to all students, especially those who have difficulty making sense of the available resource books. Another resource is speakers from the community who are invited as "experts" on the subject under study. Beforehand, we discuss the kinds of questions we need to ask these experts, and then find out as much as possible in interviews with them (Graves, 1989b).

The process may take longer than the time traditionally allotted for unit studies. Provide time! Only by thoroughly exploring the process from beginning to end can students become independent, self-directed learners. One unit studied in depth is worth any number of units in which students only skim the surface.

Responding to Fiction

Teachers consolidate oral responses to shared reading and express them in written form. These may be rewritten summaries of retellings, problems, solutions, lessons, plot lines, character interactions, and character analyses. The written response is a concise restatement of the most profound ideas reached in discussion, in which we use the exact words of students as much as possible.

We like to stretch students' thinking beyond their current reading to a comparison with other stories they have read. The three stories *The Painter and the White Swans* (Clement, 1986), *Liang and the Magic Paintbrush* (Demi, 1980), and *The Legend of the Indian Paintbrush* (de Paola, 1988) have in common a hero who is a painter. There is also an element of magic in each story. Each story, however, is set in a different country and that alone affects the layout, the illustrations, and the storyline. The following comparison was developed by Mayling and her third and fourth grade students.

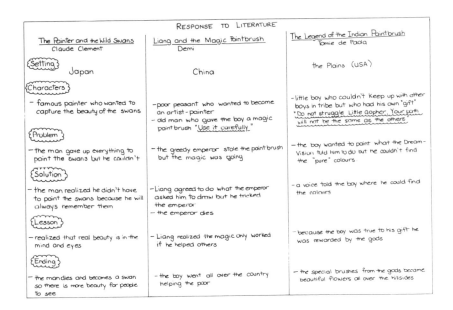

RESPONSE TO LITERATURE		
The Painter and the Wild Swans Claude Clement	Liang and the Magic Paintbrush Demi	The Legend of the Indian Paintbrush Tomie de Paola
{Setting} Japan	China	the Plains (USA)
{Characters} — famous painter who wanted to capture the beauty of the swans	— poor peasant who wanted to become an artist - painter — old man who gave the boy a magic paintbrush "Use it carefully."	— little boy who couldn't keep up with other boys in tribe but who had his own "gift" "Do not struggle Little Gopher. Your path will not be the same as the others
{Problem} — the man gave up everything to paint the swans but he couldn't	— the greedy emperor stole the paintbrush but the magic was going	— the boy wanted to paint what the Dream-Vision told him to do but he couldn't find the "pure" colours.
{Solution} — the man realized he didn't have to paint the swans because he will always remember them	— Liang agreed to do what the emperor asked him to draw but he tricked the emperor — the emperor dies	— a voice told the boy where he could find the colours
{Lesson} — realized that real beauty is in the mind and eyes	— Liang realized the magic only worked if he helped others	— because the boy was true to his gift he was rewarded by the gods
{Ending} — the man dies and becomes a swan so there is more beauty for people to see	— the boy went all over the country helping the poor	— the special brushes from the gods became beautiful flowers all over the hillsides

Revising and Editing

One way we demonstrate specific editing strategies is in the final rereading of the morning chalkboard message. Sometimes we discover the message lacks clarity, has awkwardly worded sentences, or contains errors in spelling or punctuation. We encourage students to "help us" revise or edit sections of the writing as needed. Through this activity, students learn that there is more than one way to express an idea, and that writing can be reworked in much the same way as plasticine or clay can.

We also demonstrate revising and editing strategies using examples of former students' writing. We use an overhead projector to show the writing to the class. Then we invite them to help revise and then edit parts of the writing. The class considers how the writer presented ideas and they discuss alternatives for such areas as: the introductory sentence, organization, and supporting details. We also teach specifics of punctuation, paragraphing, and tenses, using examples as discussed above.

Lists, Letters, Articles, Advertisements, Messages

When students see themselves as writers, they find many opportunities for written communication, and they use a variety of forms. Writers learn the most and do their best work if the writing is for a real (genuine) audience and is purposeful. Young children frequently model adult behavior by making shopping lists and writing notices during play. Roger made a rocket ship out of cardboard tubing at home, and proudly brought it to school to show his classmates. He set it on a display table for others to see, but he also politely warned them not to touch it.

Pleses do NoT Tuch. The rokiT.

Please do not touch the rocket.

Joy's observations as teacher researcher show that early primary students often incorporate literacy play into their free time activities if materials are handy. They need a readily available supply of crayons, and felt pens, and a variety of paper in different sizes. One student, near the end of her first year at school, wrote her perception of the classroom rules.

Classroom Rules

1. Never run in the Classroom
2. Don't Wast your time for Reading
3. No pushing or hitting
4. NO Scredlieing on Other Challderens Work
5. When it is time to Read your Reader NO yelleing forg Wred you put up your hand.
6. When the teacher is Reading a Story Don4 ful around.
7. Never trie to think that you are the Vary Best. Writer becouse it hearts the kides feeling
8. Never be Self.
9. if you Want to talk to the teacher put up your hand.
10. Don't Bouther Other kides When they are Working
11. Don't Deslerve the teacher When She is Wonking Wite the Other kides
12. and Never fight
13. and Don4 Whien

1. Never run in the classroom.
2. Don't waste your time for reading.
3. No pushing or hitting.
4. No scribbling on other children's work.
5. When it is time to read your reader, no yelling for a word. You put up your hand.
6. When the teacher is reading a story, don't fool around.
7. Never try to think that you are the very best writer because it hurts the other kids' feelings.
8. Never be selfish.
9. If you want to talk to the teacher, put up your hand.
10. Don't bother other kids when they are working.
11. Don't disturb the teacher when she is working with the other kids.
12. And never fight.
13. And don't whine.

Letters or notes that students write may be personal or general, and of all types (thank you's, news, congratulations). Berta wrote the following note of apology to her mother.

Mom, today I learned about feelings and I want to say I'm sorry when I broke the lamp. I know how you felt. It's OK. Anyway, Dad bought a new one — way over there (in her illustration).

For many years children have been communicating by writing notes during class. Joy has intercepted many of these notes, but her favorite is an exchange between a first grade boy and girl who were clearly writing for a purpose.

BOY: ~~I MIT MIRY~~

GIRL: DO YOV HADT ME
iT DUT MADr
Be KUS I DO

BOY: YES I LOvEYou

GIRL: I Mit LOVEYou

BOY: I wohtt oMirYyou

GIRL: HAFto WAt   tL yoy
r OLDr Lik 20 owr
30

BOY: TAt is
Off KA

BOY: I might marry you.
GIRL: Do you hate me?
   It doesn't matter
   because I do.
BOY: Yes, I love you.
GIRL: I might love you.
BOY: I want to marry you.
GIRL: Have to wait until you
   are older, like 20 or 30.
BOY: That is OK.

Students and teachers can converse with each other by writing notes, which they pin to a classroom message board. We choose a place for our bulletin board that is accessible to all and provide the necessary notepads, pencils (on a string), and tacks. The purpose is written communication that is authentic and interesting. We take note of the messages on the board, and do a general cleanup once a month. The message board is truly effective when we take an active part in using it ourselves.

MESSAGE BOARD COMMUNICATIONS

Wording and spelling are as written.

Example A: A plea and a promise.

To Ms. Chow

Me and Skyler think that we are abil
to sit together again.

From Anna and Skyler

Dear Anna and Skyler,

Let's try it this week. If I don't have to
remind you two to get down to work
all week, then you may move back
together. Does this sound fair?

Ms. Chow

Example B: Making arrangements

To William
From Jason

William do you want to come to my house
after your day-care and then we can
play on my sega?

To Jason

Maybe I can. It depends on what my
my mom says.

From William

Example C: A series of letters about books (and birthdays)

From a student whose first language is English (Keith) to one who is learning English as a second language (Geln.) About the book *50 Below Zero* by Robert Munsch.

To: Geln

I thought that this book is a good book because it is very funny. I thought that it was funny because Jason's father keeps on getting up. I also like the illustrations.

Dear Keith,

I haven't read this book but it seems that you like it. My favourite corector is Robert Munsch, is yours? Well, I'll hear about it. Buy.

From Geln!!!

To: Geln

Yes, my favourite athor is Robert Munsch. He is very funny. Did you know that his birthday is right before mine?

From Keith

Dear Keith

I didn't know when Robert Munche's was and I never knew it was on the same day as yours, but it was exciting to know. Oh and please tell me when the birthdays are:!?

from Geln Yo-man

To Capodray (*compadre*)

Robert Munche's birthday is on June 11th. Mine is on June 12. Neat eh? When is your birthday? By for now capodray.

From Keith

●

Do not confine your program to a limited type of writing experience. Make sure students participate in, and therefore experience, all aspects of writing.

Through shared writing we create many opportunities for students to experience writing for a multiplicity of purposes. We demonstrate the selection of topics, how writers go about developing and organizing topics, and composing strategies in general. We also focus on the mechanics involved in writing. Thus the traditional "subjects" of spelling, handwriting, printing, grammar, and language use become part of shared writing experiences.

We do not expect students to produce independently what they have not experienced in a shared situation. And some students need a number of demonstrations and opportunities to participate in a group before they internalize procedures and expectations. On the other hand we use our observations of their independent work as a major determinant for the focus of our shared sessions.

. . . .

EVALUATION

Evaluation Appropriate to Our Goals

We have written about the considerable and significant advances that have been made in understanding the nature of literacy and how it is learned. We base our evaluation on the same goals and principles that we pursue in our teaching program, in keeping with a view of learning as a developmental process of successive approximations (page 11). Therefore one of our guiding principles is to undertake evaluation individually and over time. We also want to evaluate our teaching programs and student learning in terms of what we actually value. Therefore we evaluate progress within the complete processes of reading and writing, rather than relying on inferences made just from the products. Such evaluations are integral to all our teaching, and enhance rather than restrict learning.

To be consistent with our goals, we devise and use literacy evaluation that is developmentally and culturally appropriate, genuine in nature, inclusive of a variety or range of literacy purposes, purposeful to the learners, and directly connected to the teaching program. We plan ways to facilitate self-evaluation by students. We want evaluation to augment our ability as teachers to become informed reflective observers who use ongoing evaluation as a vital source of information from which to revise and refine short-term and long-term plans. We take an active role in explaining this perspective to parents, administrators, and policy makers.

Much of our evaluation is observational, based on process even more than on product, and qualitative rather than quantitative. Thus we have developed a comprehensive understanding of what we want to accomplish and how to recognize it. We developed this understanding through observations and interactions with our students, reflections on our experiences, and study and discussions with our peers.

Throughout this book we have talked about the importance of students' enjoyment, interest, and positive feelings towards literacy and learning in general. Our goals reflect our concern with both the affective and cognitive domain. For example, we not only want our students to be able to read; we also want them to choose to read. In this way they will take ownership of, and responsibility for, their learning. Thus a number of evaluative questions we ask ourselves reflect a concern with student attitude.

Questions We Ask Ourselves

About Writing

1. Are our students writing more — longer compostions, more frequently, more fluently?
2. Are they writing for more audiences in terms of content, language, and illustrations?
3. Are they developing an authentic voice?
4. Is their sentence structure increasingly varied?
5. Can they find things to write about?
6. Can they use writing to learn, to classify thought?
7. Are they learning to revise and rewrite in order to discover what they have to say?
8. Are they learning to take ownership of their writing? (Adapted from Crowhurst, 1988.)

About Reading

1. Are our students reading more?
2. Are they choosing different kinds of books and materials to read?
3. Do they share and discuss their reading with others?
4. Do they show an intrinsic interest in books, in reading? Do they sometimes read by choice?
5. Do they select appropriate material to read (in terms of interest, difficulty, variety)?

6. Do they read to learn?
7. Are they learning how to read effectively and efficiently with a balanced set of strategies that include prior knowledge and multilevel language cue systems (semantic, syntactic, graphophonic)?

Evaluation and the Framework of Shared Components

In this chapter we discuss evaluation within the framework of the four components of the program. We ask two separate though closely connected questions. The first question concerns evaluation of our teaching strategies: How well is the program working for us? The second question involves the evaluation of student learning: How well are our students progressing?

First we consider the components in which we demonstrate the process and invite students to participate. During these activities we observe students and ask ourselves: Are these students "with us" in spirit as well as body, or are they just putting in time? But we also observe individual response. We ask: Just who is "with us" and who is not?

The answers have different impacts on us and the program. We need a positive response to the first question in order to carry out our agenda at all. If we find we are not connecting with some students, we respond in two ways. One, we try to adapt our materials and procedures to connect with these students during shared activities. (However, in so doing, we take care not to lose other students.) Two, we support students individually during independent reading and writing. Our objective is to help them build the confidence, knowledge, and understanding they need to connect with the group.

Evaluation of Shared Reading

We choose certain selections for shared reading, but do we make good choices? To evaluate our selections we observe students' responses to the materials, both during the demonstrations and later on. For example, we look to see which selections they choose to reread on their own, and which they borrow for reading at home.

We introduce reading by connecting with students' understanding and background knowledge. We gauge our success by their enthusiasm in relating to the selection, and then by the range and depth of ideas that they share with group.

During reading we want students actively listening and thinking. To judge how well students are progressing, we observe each student as we read, trying to reach students as individuals. When they take part as readers, we look for confidence and enthusiasm. If we feel restlessness or inattention on their part, we may pause for interpretation and prediction. We may even discontinue the reading at that time, and turn to subjects that seem closer to our students' concerns. When we read together, we insist that students attend to the reader and listen to the reading. Thus we show our respect for literature and its value in our lives.

We try to guide the discussions that accompany and follow reading to illuminate the reading and challenge students' thinking. When all students are willing, even eager to share, we know we have succeeded. We see them building on each other's ideas and going beyond what we expected. We also find ideas introduced in this setting spilling over into students' independent writing and their independent responses to reading. Once we feel students are responding confidently and can express and substantiate their opinions, we lead them towards evaluating responses in relation to those expressed by others. However, if student participation falls off at this point, we also know we have gone too far too fast, so we fall back to earlier strategies.

Evaluation of Shared Writing

The first level of evaluation is related to meaning and story format, our first priority (page 40). If students don't connect with the meaning of the shared writing, we conclude that either something is wrong with the message (it may be uninteresting or obscure), or with our means of presenting it (students may be unsure of their responsibilities and/or our objectives).

Next we evaluate their responses at the level of English grammar, using the shared writing to demonstrate sequence and cohesion in paragraphs, sentence units, and punctuation (page 40). We evaluate our success at this second level by observing students' ability to understand and relate to our strategies, by analyzing their independent writing, by listening as they discuss their strategies and decisions, and by asking probing questions. We revisit them regularly in the realization that students vary greatly in the point at which they can capitalize on these aspects.

The third priority is at the level of word units (page 41). It concerns decisions on vocabulary, spelling, handwriting (or printing), and proofreading in general. We demonstrate and discuss conventions of the written language system and evaluate our success by students' responses to questions and discussions, and in their use of the conventions in independent writing.

When we write chalkboard messages, we expect students to read, and sometimes to compose right along with us. We hear their spontaneous reactions to the meaning and also note their attention to form.

One morning Mayling casually commented to her class that her message was particularly boring. Her students immediately picked up the cue and offered suggestions for improvement! On another morning a first grade girl in Joy's room pointed out that a number of words in the chalkboard message were written together, without spacing. She asked why there were not spaces between *snow* and *flakes*, and between *out* and *side*. Joy, of course, seized the teachable moment and introduced the idea of compound words. She asked her students to find other examples in the morning message. She underlined these compound words. When writing independently later that day, four students competently used compound words and indicated their intention by underlining them also.

In this way our professional observations immediately translate into significant teaching and are extended in turn into careful observations of students' responses to such teaching. We record these events in anecdotal notes, which form the raw data for our evaluation.

Goals of Evaluating Independent Components

When students read and write independently, they show what strategies and knowledge they can apply on their own. Their reading and writing provide a window through which we can infer and then discuss their understanding. We can discover if they have internalized the strategies we have demonstrated in our shared sessions. Therefore the progress we see in students' independent reading and writing provides both a measure of the success of those sessions and diagnostic information that may determine the focus of future sessions.

Independent Reading: A Qualitative Perspective

We present a procedure of miscue analysis that gives a very detailed picture of strategies readers are using once they are working at applying their awareness of sound-letter correspondences. We are not suggesting that teachers follow this procedure with all students. We examine the reading in such detail only when we have special concerns. The importance of this qualitative analysis is the view it gives us of the nature and complexity of the reading process. We internalize the framework and thus are able to intelligently observe the strategies our readers are using. We can then coach and evaluate them over time.

Our procedure is based on a much more complex one, the *Reading Miscue Inventory* (Y. Goodman and C. Burke, 1972). It analyzes the cue systems that readers use simultaneously at three different levels of language. First is the semantic cue system, which deals with whether the miscue makes sense in the sentence as well as in the story as a whole. Second is the grammatical cue system, which deals with the grammaticality of the miscue in the sentence. Third is the graphophonic cue system, which deals with the correspondence of patterns of sounds (phonemes) to the correspondence of patterns of letters (graphemes) at the word level.

PROCEDURE DURING READING

We preselect three books that seem appropriate to the readers. We chat briefly to make them feel comfortable and then explain the procedure as follows:

> Have a look at these three books and choose one to read out loud. I will tape your reading so we can listen to some of it and talk about it afterwards. I won't need to help you because I know you have found ways to keep on reading when you read alone. I will ask you to tell me the story in your own words afterwards.

During the reading we make encouraging supportive sounds or comments about the student's reading strategies, but do not correct his or her reading. We might say, "Mmm-hmm," or "Oh, good correcting!" If the student pauses or hesitates, we might say, "Ah, you noticed something!" When the student has read the entire selection (a vital aspect), we shift into the retelling procedure.

We record the miscues, or deviations from the text, on a pre-pared worksheet, as in the example below, using the code of marks indicated. By recording the miscues in this way, we can study their characteristics in detail and evaluate how effectively readers are integrating the use of the language cue systems into a balanced whole.

Miscue Marking Code

Gurglebell Grumble	Substitution written above in longhand.
$\wedge$	Insertion — of word or inferred punctuation mark, marked by a caret.
(mean)	Circle omission — of word(s) or punctuation mark.
I'll go home	Underline — rereading.
c Then Grumble ran	Underline and mark with c the miscue successfully corrected by rereading.
uc to dig with	Underline and mark with uc, unsuccessful correction attempt by rereading.
an elf always/has	Slash mark denotes pause in reading.

An Example

The following example is the result of a consultation between Marietta and Sue, a third grade student who arrived late in the school year and was repeating the grade. Her parents were much concerned about her slow progress in the regular classroom and her new classroom teacher wanted to determine an appropriate program for her.

Miscue Worksheet for *The Pot of Gold* (Scott Foresman Publishers, 1976).

Text with Marked Miscues	Discussion of Some Numbered Miscues
1. Once upon a time there was a / (mean) man	1. Sue, the reader, omitted *mean*, but in her retelling (see below) she specifically called this character mean.

2. Gurglebell

2. named Grumble.

Gurglebell was 3.

3. One day Grumble saw an elf in the woods.

Gurglebell 4. *was*

4. Grumble said, "An elf always has *had* 5.

5. a pot of gold.

6. his

6. I'll make this elf take

7. me to his pot of gold."

Gurglebell

8. Grumble took hold of the elf.

his

9. The elf began to jerk this way and

10. that way. *Gurglebell*

11. But Grumble didn't let go.

12. The elf said, "Let me go! Let me go!"

Gurglebell

13. Grumble said, "Take me to your pot of gold.

14. Then I'll let you go." *Gurglebell*

15. The elf took Grumble to a big tree.

16. The elf said, "The gold is under this tree.

©7. *be*

17. You'll have to dig deep to get it."

Gurglebell

18. Grumble said, "I'll need a shovel ©3 *big*

© *with* ac 2 *bu-ig*

1 *bring*

19. to dig with.

20. I'll go home and get one.

© *m-*

21. But first I'll mark the tree so I can

22. find it again."

90

2. Gurglebell is the name that Sue settles on to use throughout the reading — but although she has thereby lost out on this clue, she clearly expresses this understanding as well.

4. *Had* for *has*, although grammatically close, caused a very significant loss of meaning as revealed in the retelling.

6. Miscue *his* for *this*, although semantically and grammatically fine, creates an unusual phrase, which is left, probably through overreliance on graphophonics.

17. *Be* for *dig* is the first of many attempted corrections.

19. Miscue *big* for *dig*. The first attempt is of the same part of speech. Second and third efforts use phonics without success.

Gurglebell
23. Grumble took off his red
    ⓒ *the* scarf and put it
    ⓒ *his*
24. on a branch of the tree.
    ⓒ
25. He said, ⁽¹¹⁾Now promise you
    won't take

26. my scarf off the tree."

27. The elf said, "I promise."
    Gurglebell
28. Grumble let the elf go.
    ⓒ *The Gurglebell*
29. Then Grumble ran home to
    get a shovel. ⓒ *12. I'll*
    Gurglebell
30. Grumble said, "Now all I
    have to do is
    ⓒ *big*
31. dig up the gold, and I'll be
    rich."
    14. Then Gurglebell
32. When Grumble got back, he
    took looked for
    16. has
33. the tree that had his red scarf
    on it.
    17. keeped
34. The elf had kept his promise.
    ⓒ *18. got*   *19. Gurglebell's*
35. He had not taken Grumble's
    scarf

36. off the tree.

37. He had put a red scarf on
    every tree.
    Gurglebell
38. Grumble began to yell and
    scream and
    20. stump ⓒ *a 21.*
39. stamp his feet.

40. But that didn't help at all.
    22. ⓒ *dig*
41. So he began to dig, and he
    may still

42. be digging.

31. This time Sue read past the repeated miscue *big* for *dig*, which did not fit semantically or grammatically. This simultaneous dissonance created a strong need and source of correction.

41., 42. Here Sue appropriately predicted that Gurglebell continued to dig but used the following print to disconfirm her prediction of the wording and then to reread and self-correct.

91

At the beginning of the story, Sue makes several miscues, which she leaves uncorrected. However, her hesitations are significant because they indicate that she is aware of problems and therefore must be attending to meaning. In such instances, encourage readers to go back and self-correct any problems that they notice.

In lines 9 through 16, there are no miscues other than *Gurglebell*. Fluency and context are now building as the writer's options are decreasing. Perhaps Sue is also becoming convinced that Marietta really will not interrupt or help her. By line 17, Sue is well into the story and it becomes clear that she is actively predicting as she reads, forming and testing her hypotheses concerning meaning, grammar, and wording of the story. At this point she makes the first of several corrections.

Correction strategies are highly significant in the reading process. Once we see readers self-correcting, we know they are beginning to cross-check their use of the cue systems against one another, making judgments and then working at integrating their use. If we prompt or correct readers, we are interfering with the development of this important strategy. We are also taking away their control over the process, which implies that we do not believe they can handle it.

Sue's reading clearly reveals that she is operating with the same processes and strategies as able readers. She is using a multitude of strategies along with interacting cue systems at the various language levels, and is fitting these together with her background knowledge and the picture cues. What Sue lacks is proficiency in integrating their use in an efficient, balanced way. Such proficiency develops within the complete process where the reader's focus is genuinely upon re-creating meaning.

PROCEDURE FOLLOWING READING

To examine Sue's comprehension of the story as a whole, Marietta asked her to retell it, also using a simplified format based on the Reading Miscue Inventory (Y. Goodman and C. Burke, 1972). This procedure involves requesting a spontaneous retelling and then pursuing it with a guided retelling to elicit additional information and to clarify questions arising from the reading. The significant portion of this conversation is transcribed below.

Transcript of Retelling

M. = Marietta.   S. = Sue.

M: Now tell me about this story.
S: Gurglebell was trying to find gold by the little elf because he — he saw the little elf with the gold so he wanted it. And the elf kept his promise but he done — um, — he put — every — every scarf on the tree, so Gurglebell wouldn't know which one it was.
M: Mm-hm.
S: So he kept on digging and digging.
M: Mm-hm. Right.

Guided Retelling Section

M: Tell me what the problem in the story was.
S: That Gurglebell couldn't find the gold.
M: Did he solve his problem?
S: No.
M: Was there a lesson in the story?
S: Yes.
M: Tell me about it.
S: You won't get anything if you cry and stamp your feet.
M: (laughing) Mm-hm. Tell me about Gurglebell.
S: He was big and he was mean (see miscue 1), and he tried to get rich but he couldn't.

In her retelling Sue revealed that she followed the basic plot, and was able to draw a conclusion on the theme from her point of view. She understood many aspects that she did not correct in her reading, particularly near the beginning of the story. Sue was able to go on to describe the scene and to tell more about the characters. She also explained that she realized Gurglebell was not the actual name of Grumble, but she could not "sound out" the word. She was clearly able to recreate the basic meaning of the story so that it made sense from her perspective. This reading was therefore genuinely purposeful to her.

A summary of Sue's reading and comprehension indicates that she is working on integrating her strategies to make sense of the story. Thus our evaluation indicates she is well on her way to becoming an effective reader.

Data for Individual Reader Profiles

Our goal is to enable students to see themselves as readers who read effectively for their own purposes and enjoyment. Thus, in addition to our observations of reading strategies, we note how they are approaching reading. Their confidence, their enthusiasm, the difficulty and familiarity of their selections, and their discussions about the meaning of their reading are all indicators of the effectiveness of their reading.

This data forms the profile of each individual reader, which we file in an individual portfolio, along with anecdotal comments and any tapes or transcripts we may have. We make a particular point to record and keep tapes of students who are developing slowly or have experienced more than average difficulty. These provide us with evidence to support our evaluation of their competencies.

What we must do is internalize the qualitative framework described above so we can make informed observations of readers' strategies without going through the whole procedure. We are then in a position to collect data to form successive profiles and evaluate progress.

Evaluation Strategies: Early Primary

We designed the Record of Reading Strategies to summarize data on the reading of our early primary students. We record what they know about book handling (how they open a book, the way they turn the pages, the order in which they read pages facing one another). We also note how or if they track the print and if they match their oral renditions to it. We note when they start matching words as units and attending to first letters in words.

A significant shift occurs once students consistently focus on the print, and work on integrating their knowledge of the system of letter-sound correspondences with their use of illustrations, meaning, and grammar. At this point we focus our observations on their relative use of the language cue systems. Which do they use as their major sources of prediction and of self-correction — confirmation or disconfirmation? What strategies do they use when they are having problems? Do they come to a halt, seek help, reread, or read on to pick up more context? How flexible are their strategies? What success are they having in developing independent reading strategies? How fluently do they read? We pay particular attention to the progress of our young readers in integrating strategies, and to the relative balance they are achieving.

We use the following record to keep track of our students' strategies and to record the date on which we first notice new strategies appearing.

Do not use such a record to determine any sequence of teaching various aspects, but as a way of simplifying the recording of the strategies you observe.

Record of Reading Strategies

Name _____   Date _____

BOOK HANDLING
Direction of pages _____
Pages in sequence _____
Left to right page sequence _____

TRACKING PRINT
Sweep with finger _____
Word by word — finger _____
                        — voice _____

MATCHING ORAL TO PRINT
Oral to illustrations only _____
Begins with print _____
Ends with print _____
Matching words as units _____
Attention to first letters _____
Single words identified _____
Comments _____
_____

ALPHABETIC STRATEGIES
Sounds aloud _____
Use of meaning _____
Use of grammar _____
Use of letter-sound _____
Use of illustrations _____

Asks for a word _____

Self-correction _____

Integration/balance of strategies _____

Rereading own writing _____

We keep these forms in students' individual portfolios and evaluate progress by examining changes over time. The portfolios also contain anecdotal notes on significant observations made in shared reading sessions, and teacher/student conferences. We comment on the fluency of students' readings, and their use of strategies. We note which strategies they control, which they are working on applying in their individual work, and which they are managing to apply with group or teacher support. We also note the type, level, and familiarity of the material in which they demonstrate these competencies.

Reports to parents of early primary students

Primary reading is generally anecdotal in nature and relies heavily on teacher/parent interviews. We focus on students' strengths and give some indication of what we expect from them. Some sample comments are:

1. Dennis reads fluently, using a balance of strategies to work out new words independently. He is enjoying the challenge of reading from a wide variety of books.
2. Beverly is now reading a variety of children's literature and books containing factual information. She has a good memory for details and enjoys comparing versions of the same fairytale.
3. Avi is adjusting nicely to the classroom routine. He is enjoying the beginning reading activities and seems eager to learn to read. He prints a few words by sight and uses sight-sound correspondences to write and reread his writing. Thus I expect he will soon be deciphering the text in books.

Evaluation Strategies: Late Primary and Intermediate

At the intermediate level, we continue to base our evaluation on the same qualitative aspects that we use at the primary level. We continue to focus on what students can do and are trying to do. We include observations of the product, as well as the process, by including data that we glean from analyzing oral reading, retellings, and discussions and entries that students make in their reading logs and journals. We use our individual conference time to carefully observe and note key findings on the Teacher Conference Record. Some sample findings are:

- Skipping over difficult words; choice much too difficult. Discuss strategies and choice.
- Substituting words that make sense, but too difficult a choice. Sent back to select another book.
- Oral retelling is sequential and detailed, but has trouble generalizing a lesson.
- Fine retelling and comparison with story of Cinderella.
- Oral reading OK. Retelling too detailed. Monitor for summarizing.

Certain external demands require us to supply comparisons of our students or to determine a "grade level." To meet these requests, we ask our students to choose a story to read from a graded basal reader or we administer any required district or provincial, standardized tests. However, we take care to base the bulk of our evaluation on complete selections, across a range of reading purposes in which our readers are genuinely involved.

Keep in mind that evaluation inevitably determines and drives the curriculum.

Evaluation of Independent Writing: Early Primary

We want our students, first of all, to see themselves as writers. Thus we observe their attitudes, their ability to choose topics of interest to them, and their fluency in developing those topics. Such observations are subjective in nature and become part of our working picture of our class. We also evaluate students' progress as writers by analyzing the strategies they use to compose and transcribe their writing, and by observing changes over time.

We evaluate students' composing strategies at the three levels of priority previously discussed. We insist, first of all, that the message makes sense to the writer, and then that the writer can explain it to the reader. The movement is toward decontextualized writing that delivers a meaning that can stand on its own.

At the second level we evaluate students' use of language. We view growth as a progression from "talk written down" to using conventions of written language. We look for wording that is a genuine reflection of the writer's voice; that is, not copied either directly or from memory. We look for increasing complexity of ideas, length, and variety of form. When we evaluate at the level of word representation, we use the five levels of development described on pages 30–34. These levels are on our minds as we observe our young writers on a day-to-day basis, and they enable us to analyze both process and product. We note changes in strategies at the backs of students' writing books, and use these notes as a main source of material for evaluation.

The Record of Writing Strategies provides a way of summarizing each student's progress. Lee suggests using one form per student per year, marking the date or otherwise noting when students incorporate the characteristics into their writing. One approach to summarizing progress is to scan the back pages of students' writing books to bring all lists up to date at regular intervals (perhaps once every six to eight weeks). Another approach is to note when significant changes appear; for example, a student's first attempt to map letters to sounds.

The order of the items tends to be sequential. However, we don't expect all students to progress in the same fashion, nor do we expect all writers to show every characteristic. We keep the form, along with significant examples of students' writing, in their portfolios. The record focuses our observations and summarizes individual writers' strengths and progress.

Record of Writing Strategies

Transcription

PREPHONETIC

Cursive-like _____

Letters — upper case _____

      — lower case _____

_____

Prints own name _____

Copies _____

Relates message — to drawing _____

            — to writing _____

Indicates letter(s) stand for word unit _____

SEMIPHONETIC

Uses specific letter(s) to stand for perceived sound(s) _____
Sounds through the message during writing _____
Rereads in process _____
Represents — beginning and final consonants _____
        — most consonants _____
        — long vowels _____
Reads match between oral and written language _____

PHONETIC

Indicates word boundaries _____
Conventional word separation _____
Represents — short vowels _____
        — most surface sounds _____
Edits during reading _____

TRANSITIONAL

Visual approximations _____
Sight words _____
Conventional short vowels _____
Inflected patterns (*ed, ing*) _____

Composition

Labels/names _____
Journal _____
Retells a familiar story _____
Story _____
Information-giving _____

Keep in mind that progress is not necessarily regular or linear. Our experience is that it follows an upward spiral, with writers focusing their energy first on one aspect, and then another.

Reporting to Parents of Primary Students

The Record of Writing Strategies provides a qualitative framework for observing students' progress. However, we do not use it as an instrument for reporting to parents or other agencies. Comments we have used on anecdotal reports include:

1. Sheila is willing to take risks. She can now read back the interesting stories that she writes each day using her own spellings.
2. Billy knows a number of letter-sound correspondences, but he is not yet using them in his daily story-writing. He has a lot of good ideas, but seems reluctant to take the risk of making a mistake.
3. Mako is writing wonderful stories. She seems very confident about writing down her ideas, and her spelling is becoming quite conventional.

Evaluation of Independent Writing: Late Primary and Intermediate

When we conference student writing, we focus attention on the meaning and the strengths of a piece. However, we also carefully observe and recognize the strategies a writer is using to make his or her point. Albert, the writer of the following selection, has been writing regularly on topics of his own choice. Lee's observations indicate that he is writing fluently, with little interruption. The following example is one of his first drafts, reproduced line by line as written. Lee's analysis appears on the right.

LocKed in a chasl.

1. One day my firind and I sow	Setting, main characters.
2. a chasl. We dside to go in	Initiating event.
3. the chasl. As soon as we got	
4. in the jobrig wint up.	Problem #1.
5. So I went up to the top.	Solution #1.
6. And looked and sow an	
7. alagater. So we dind jump.	Solution didn't work.
8. We dside to Look down	
9. stars for a way out.	Solution #2.
10. And we didn't. Thin ouL of	Solution didn't work.
11. a sudin a big dragon came	
12. up from under neth the	Problem #2.
13. brich flor. Thin it disod	
14. peard into thin air. Thin	A red herring!
15. we herd something comeing	Problem #3.
16. It sounid like horse	Suspense!
17. We had to haid But	
18. ware? Thin I said up	Solution #3.

19. stars. I said to my
20. friend. And my friend
21. said what a Buot up stars   Prolonging the suspense.
22. and I said we can haid
23. up stars. Ant he said no
24. if we haid down stars
25. we can run out Bneth   Solution #4.
26. thir lag's and we did.   A successful climax!

Albert's short piece has the elements of a conventional adventure story. His opening sentence tells us when the story happened, who the main characters are, and the facts about the setting. Then he immediately propels his characters into the action; the "drawbridge goes up" and they meet their first problem. The story continues with a series of problems that occur within the larger problem of finding a means of escape. Some problems are solved and some are not.

Albert uses several stylistic devices for interest and effect: conversation between the main characters, problems that turn out not to be problems (red herrings), and wording that heightens the tension and prolongs the suspense. Finally the story reaches its climax and quickly comes to a tidy conclusion.

Albert has written a story that is cohesive, clear, and sequentially laid out. We can imagine the events even though we do not have quite all the details. We can also see the underlying themes of curiosity leading to danger, the value of courage and persistence, and the benefit gained by working cooperatively. Therefore we can say Albert meets readers' needs at the level of meaning (our first priority).

At the second level of grammar and structure, we can applaud Albert's organization and his control over grammatical construction. We note that he can produce the tone of narration and direct speech. He shows an awareness of sentence units, using periods conventionally up to line 15, but with omissions from that point on (perhaps he was concentrating on working out the plot). We would expect that he could easily provide the necessary periods prior to publication. The direct quotations are not marked and so it is appropriate to consider these for future demonstration and discussion.

The third priority is at the level of words. While Albert has incorporated a number of relatively mature strategies into his composition, we can see that he is still at a transitional level in spelling. His approximations are visual (*firind, dind*) and phonetic (*jobrig, bneth*). We want him to make judgments concerning his spelling and to develop his awareness of conventions, so we ask him to circle the words he feels he needs help with. Then we print them in conventional form (for example, *castle* = *chasl*), perhaps with some explanation (for example, the *draw* in *drawbridge*). We note that Albert is working on -*ed* and -*ing* endings.

Such an analysis reveals students' functional levels and suggests areas of focus for future shared sessions. The trick is to encourage students to incorporate language conventions at all levels without inhibiting their desire to write.

Be knowledgeable about writing development and what is typical of students at particular ages. Monitor each writer's progress and then exercise judgment to decide when it is time to nudge and when it is time to leave well enough alone.

Data for Individual Writing Profiles

Our students keep all their writing in a folder along with a record form of titles, dates, and conferencing points (page 37). We examine the contents at regular intervals to observe and interpret patterns of growth at all three levels of priority (pages 40–41). We may photocopy significant pieces of writing to keep in students' portfolios along with anecdotal notes and other examples of their work (including any test results). Our Teacher's Conference Record (page 37) is a day-to-day record of students' writing and our responses to it. It is, therefore, another valuable source of evaluative data. We make notations such as the following:

- Discussed story problem orally; check inclusion in writing tomorrow.
- Ready to organize facts (cut and paste).
- Why did rat get more votes? Clarify ending.
- Inconsistent spelling strategies; therefore difficult to read. *Monitor progress.

As our students' writing matures, we expect them to be able to polish first drafts and prepare final copies. We then ask students to submit this writing for marks. We evaluate the writing holistically, using the following ratings:

- 5 Superior: well above average at all three levels of priority (meaning, grammar, and word usage).
- 4 Commendable: in reasonable control of the priorities.
- 3 Improvement Needed: functional in terms of priority 1, but in need of revision and editing.
- 2 Minimal: ideas and information are present, but the writing lacks clarity and cohesion (priority 1).
- 1 Insufficient Material: explanations and clarification restricted to oral responses.

Once we begin such a marking system, we need to use it regularly; for example, once a month. We can also apply it to the written components of reports in subject areas. Marking students' writing put us in the role of "judges" who assess excellence, whereas before we were in the role of "mentors" who assist improvement. The circumstances of this shift in roles must be clear in the minds of students and teachers, or the whole mentoring process will break down.

We are well aware that the teaching profession, as a whole, has only begun to address evaluating student learning and programs in a manner consistent with the new knowledge gained from recent research in education. Our approach to evaluation is also at a formative stage. However, we cannot allow this to restrict us in incorporating significant insights we already have about learning and teaching. Teachers need the knowledge, expertise, and confidence to justify what they do and how they do it. We hope our book contributes to that body of knowledge so that other teachers, too, will have the courage to pursue that which they know is valuable for the sake of their students and themselves.

REFERENCES

Professional Books and Articles

Altwerger, B., Edelsky, C., and Flores, B. "Whole language: what's new?" *The Reading Teacher*, 41(2). (1987): 144-154.

Atwell, N. *In the middle: writing, reading, and learning with adolescents*. Montclair, NJ: Boynton-Cook, 1987.

Baskwill, J. and Whitman, P. *Evaluation: whole language, whole child*. Richmond Hill, ON: Scholastic, 1988.

Belanger, J. "Conflict between mentor and judge: being fair and being helpful in composition evaluation." *English Quarterly*, 18(4). (1985): 79-82.

Berglund, R.L. "Convention sessions address whole language evaluation." *Reading Today*, 7(3). (1989): 34.

Bissex, G.L. *Gnys at wrk: a child learns to write and read*. Cambridge, MA: Harvard University Press, 1980.

Bissex, G.L. "Watching young writers." In *Observing the language learner*. Edited by Jagger, A. and Smith-Burke, M.T. Newark, DL: International Reading Association, 1985.

Calkins, L. *Lessons from a child*. Exeter, NH: Heinemann Educational Books, 1983.

Calkins, L. *The art of teaching writing*. Exeter, NH: Heinemann Educational Books, 1986.

Cambourne, B. *The whole story*. Richmond Hill, ON: Scholastic, 1988.

Chomsky, C. "Approaching reading through invented spelling." In *Theory and practice of early reading* (Vol. 2). Edited by Resnick, L.B. and Weaver, P.A. Hillsdale, NJ: Heinemann Educational Books, 1979.

Chow, M. "Acquisition of written language by ESL children during the kindergarten and grade one years." Master's thesis. Vancouver: University of British Columbia, 1990.

Chow, M. "Nurturing the growth of writing in the kindergarten and grade one years: how are the ESL children doing?" *TESL Canada Journal*, 4(1). (1986): 35-47.

Clay, M.M. *Observing young readers*. Exeter, NH: Heinemann Educational Books, 1982.

Cohen, S.A. *Tests: marked for life?* Richmond Hill, ON: Scholastic, 1988.

Crowhurst, M. "Prerequisites for teaching writing: what the writing teacher needs to know and be." *Canadian Journal of English Language Arts*, 11(2). (1988): 5-12.

Cullinan, B.E. *Children's literature in the reading program*. Newark, DL: International Reading Association, 1987.

Dobson, L.N. "Connections in learning to write and read: a study of children's development through kindergarten and first grade." In *Reading and writing connections*. Edited by Mason, J. Needham Heights, MA: Allyn and Bacon, 1989.

Froese, V. "Assessment: form and function." In *Whole-language: practice and theory*. Edited by Froese, V. Scarborough, ON: Prentice-Hall, 1990, pp. 243-265.

Gentry, J.R. "An analysis of developmental spelling in gnys at wrk." *The Reading Teacher*, 36(2). (1982): 192-200.

Goodman, K. "Reading: the key is in children's language." *The Reading Teacher*, 25(6). (1972): 505-508.

Goodman, K. *Reading of American children whose language is a stable rural dialect of English or a language other than English*. U.S. Department of Health, Education and Welfare, National Institute of Education, Final Report, 1978 Project No. NIE-C-00-3-0087.

Goodman, K. *What's whole in whole language?* Richmond Hill, ON: Scholastic, 1986.

Goodman, K., Goodman, Y., and Hood, W. *The whole language evaluation book.* Toronto: Irwin, 1989.

Goodman, Y. and Burke, C. *Reading miscue inventory manual: procedure for diagnosis and evaluation.* New York: Macmillan, 1972.

Graves, D.H. *Writing: teachers and children at work.* Exeter, NH: Heinemann Educational Books, 1983.

Graves, D.H. *Experiment with fiction.* Exeter, NH: Heinemann Educational Books, 1989a.

Graves, D.H. *Investigate non-fiction.* Exeter, NH: Heinemann Educational Books, 1989b.

Hall, N. *The emergence of literacy.* Portsmouth, NH: Heinemann Educational Books, 1987.

Hansen, J. *When writers read.* Portsmouth, NH: Heinemann Educational Books, 1987.

Henderson, E.H. and Beers, J.W. *Developmental and cognitive aspects of learning to spell: a reflection of word knowledge.* Newark, DL: International Reading Association, 1980.

Holdaway, D. *Foundations of literacy.* Richmond Hill, ON: Scholastic, 1979.

Hurst, M. "The influence of evolving theory and practice on teaching emergent readers and writers." Master's paper. Vancouver: University of British Columbia, 1982.

Hurst, M., et al. *A program to foster literacy: early steps in learning to write.* Vancouver: B.C. Teacher's Federation, Lesson Aids #8094, 1983.

Jagger, A. and Smith-Burke, J.M. *Observing the language learner.* Newark, DL: International Reading Association, 1985.

Johnson, T. and Louis, D. *Literacy through literature.* Richmond Hill, ON: Scholastic, 1987.

Johnson, T. and Louis, D. *Bringing it all together.* Richmond Hill, ON: Scholastic, 1990.

Mickelson, N. "Recasting evaluation: centred in the classroom." Newsmagazine of the B.C. Teachers' Federation, *Teacher,* 2(3). (1989): 11-12.

Murray, D.M. *Write to learn.* (2nd ed.) New York: Holt, Rinehart and Winston, 1987.

Nathan, R., et al. *Classroom strategies that work: a guide to process writing.* Portsmouth, NH: Heinemann Educational Books, 1989.

Newman, J.M. *Whole language: theory in use.* Portsmouth, NH: Heinemann Educational Books, 1985.

Nucich, J. "An in-depth analysis of the connections between the development of letter-sound correspondence in writing and beginning reading." Master's thesis. Vancouver: University of British Colombia, 1991.

Read, C. "Preschool children's knowledge of English phonology." *Harvard Educational Review,* 41(1). (1971): 1-34.

Routman, R. *Transitions from literature to literacy.* Portsmouth, NH: Heinemann Educational Books, 1988.

Smith, F. *Reading without nonsense.* New York: Teachers College Press, 1979.

Smith F. *Schooling: an insult to the intelligence.* New York: Arbor House, 1986.

Strickland, D.S. and Mandel Morrow, L. "Assessment and early literacy." *The Reading Teacher,* 42(8). (1989): 178-179.

Taylor, D. *Family literacy: young children learning to read and write.* Portsmouth, NH: Heinemann Educational Books, 1983.

Teale, W. and Sulzby, E. *Emergent literacy.* Norwood, NJ: Ablex, 1986.

Temple, C., et al. *The beginnings of writing.* Boston, MA: Allyn and Bacon, 1982.

Valencia, S. "A portfolio approach to classroom reading assessment: the whys, whats and hows." *The Reading Teacher,* 43(4). (1990): 338-340.

Verriour, P. "Drama in the whole-language classroom." In *Whole-language: practice and theory.* Edited by Froese, V. Scarborough, ON: Prentice-Hall, 1990, pp.161-183.

Weaver, C. *Reading process and practice: from socio-psycholinguistics to whole language.* Portsmouth, NH: Heinemann Educational Books, 1988.

Children's Literature: Books and Series

Branley, F.M. *Comets*. Toronto: Fitzhenry and Whiteside, 1984.

Carlson, Nancy. *Loudmouth George and the sixth grade bully*. New York: Puffin, 1985.

Clement, C. *The painter and the wild swans*. New York: Dial, 1986.

Copp Clark. *Off to school*. London: Copp Clark, 1960.

dePaolo, T. *The legend of the Indian paintbrush*. New York: Putnam's, 1988.

Demi. *Liang and the magic paintbrush*. New York: Henry Holt, 1980.

Dobson, L. and Hurst, M. *I can read* series. Vancouver: C.R. Associates, 1980.

Hargreaves, R. *Mr. Greedy* series. London: Thurman, 1981.

Kellogg, S. *Chicken Little*. New York: Mulberry Books, 1985.

MacDonald Educational Series. *Animal world* series. London: Purnell and Sons, 1989.

Martin Jr., B. and Archambault, J. *The ghost-eye tree*. New York: Henry Holt, 1985.

Martin Jr., B. *Sounds I remember*. Toronto: Holt Rinehart and Winston, 1972.

Mayer, M. *The unicorn and the lake*. New York: Dial, 1982.

Melser, J. *Storybox* series. Auckland, New Zealand: Shortland, 1980.

Melser, J. *Little red hen*. In *Help me*. Auckland, New Zealand: Shortland, 1980.

Munsch, R. *The paper bag princess*. Toronto: Annick, 1980.

Munsch, R. *50 below zero*. Toronto: Annick, 1986.

Naden, C.J. *Perseus and Medusa*. Mahwah, NJ: Troll Associates, 1981.

Scott Foresman Publishers. *The pot of gold. Reading Unlimited* series. Glenview, IL: Scott Foresman, 1976.

Suzuki, D. with Hehner, B. *Looking at the body*. Toronto: Stoddart, 1987.

Tejima. *Fox's dream*. New York: Philomel, 1987.

Time-Life. *A child's first library of learning: how things work*. Alexandria, VA: Time-Life, 1989.

Walker, L. and Walker, H. *Classroom reader scripts*. Vancouver: Take Part Productions, 1989.

Williams, J. *Petronella*. New York: Parents Magazine Press, 1973.